Memories of United Counties
Part 1: Northampton

The *Northampton Chronicle & Echo* offices in Northampton's Market Square in the 1950s

Memories of United Counties

Reminiscences of staff past and present
compiled by Caroline Cleaveley

Part 1: Northampton

Silver Link Publishing Ltd

ISBN 978 1 85794 343 6

Silver Link Publishing Ltd
The Trundle
Ringstead Road
Great Addington
Kettering
Northants NN14 4BW

Tel/Fax: 01536 330588
email: sales@nostalgiacollection.com
Website: www.nostalgiacollection.com

Printed and bound in the Czech Republic

First published in 2010

British Library Cataloguing in Publication Data

A catalogue record for this book is available from the British Library.

Acknowledgements

I would like to thank the management and staff of Stagecoach East (United Counties) and Arriva Shires and Essex; Roger Warwick, for his historical record of United Counties and his invaluable help with this publication; Steve Loveridge, for loan of archive material and help with identifying colleagues; *Kettering Evening Telegraph*; *Northampton Chronicle and Echo*; *Bus and Coach Preservation* magazine; *Bedford on Sunday* newspaper; and Kevin Lane, for his book on United Counties.

Roger Warwick MCIT

Steve Loveridge

Kettering Evening Telegraph

Contents

Foreword

When I arrived in the hot seat of United Counties Omnibus Co Ltd in 2005 it had already been owned by Stagecoach for nearly 20 years, so I was Managing Director of what was known as 'Stagecoach East'. None the less, the Operator's Licence belonged to UCOC and that was also the legal lettering on the side of all the buses, so I felt that I was managing the real successor to the UCOC of yesteryear.

It always surprised me that, despite its size and importance, remarkably little of the history of United Counties had been written up – and yet, from what I could see, that history was every bit as significant as that of the more famous operators. So when Caroline Cleaveley approached me to see if I liked the idea of her compiling a new book on United Counties, I was delighted and happy to encourage her to get started. In 2007 I moved on to pastures new, but Caroline got into her stride and she has worked tirelessly on the project – digging out material, speaking to members of staff old and new and piecing together the story. The work that you see now, with its companion volume, is the result of all this energy and effort. It celebrates the effort and commitment of so many people who made the United Counties Omnibus Company what it was.

The book appears at a significant time, with the recent decision by Stagecoach to separate the Bedford-based operations of UCOC from the Northamptonshire core, thus effectively taking the one-time Eastern National part of United Counties on to a different destiny from the rest. How history comes round…! I welcome this book as a worthy addition to our understanding of the past and the part played by United Counties in our world.

James Freeman,
Chief Executive Officer,
Reading Transport Ltd

Introduction

All bus companies are always immortalised by the sort of buses they ran, the size of the fleet and the occasional person who was the Chief Engineer or the General Manager. But no bus company can operate without the mass of people who work as a team to make sure that a bus arrives at a bus stop at a certain time every weekday, every week of the year.

This can be summed up by Mrs B. Walton of Hitchin Depot in her poem, which appeared in the July 1977 edition of *National Bus Company News:*

> All over this fair land of ours bus fleets are on the road
> With bus crews conveying to and fro their daily loads;
> Long-distance travel coaches too, with some so dazzling bright,
> Those washing mums would term that shade a whiter white.
> The colour scheme is varied with so many on the scene;
> The green you've seen could not have been a greener green.
> Whate'er its colour, depot, town, the bus is there each day,
> Come snow, come sleet, on ploughs the fleet you're on your way.
> Delays and incidents occur from time to time, and yet
> The public know a fairer deal is hard to get.
> To serve the public really well each one must play a role;
> To keep those wheels a-turning is a worthwhile goal.
> Cooperation is the theme, for that's the only way,
> And every level works to make the service pay:
> Administration at the top and fitters in the pit,
> With countless others in between all showing grit.
> Bus-people stay for years and those with lifetime service plenty –
> This writer notches up a score, just twenty.
> Whatever the appeal can be is somehow hard to pin,
> But none the less there's something gets inside your skin –
> A different way of life perhaps – with no two days the same,
> But 'On the buses' isn't just a fancy name.
> With opportunities galore, the male myth to explode,
> The female 'mith' can also be king of the road.
> Yes! Ladies can with confidence the driving seat acquire;
> To that which once was out of bounds they now aspire.
> Aspirants are accepted with a minimum of fuss
> And veterans everywhere commend life on the bus.'

Mrs B. Walton from Hitchin (third from right) is pictured with (left to right) Doug Elphee, R. Osbourne, Tony Cassidy, J. Corbin, V. Watson, Tom White, Mrs Wheeler, Brian McCall and Len Gentle. *NBC News*

United Counties was no exception. For every bus driver and conductor there were a mass of people to back them up.

This book is a tribute to all the staff who made the United Counties bus service possible. Using interviews with current and retired staff members, I have been able to produce a picture of the work involved and the social scene that made up the bus company.

United Counties started as a service in the 1920s, mainly in the Northamptonshire area. In the 1950s it became larger as a result of amalgamation with the Western Division of Eastern National, in Bedfordshire, Buckinghamshire, Cambridgeshire, Huntingdonshire, Hertfordshire and Lincolnshire. In 1970 Luton Corporation services were amalgamated. In 1987 the company was split into three: Luton & District was formed from the Luton, Aylesbury and Hitchin areas, Milton Keynes was the second area, leaving Bedford, Biggleswade, Huntingdon, Northampton, Kettering and Corby as Stagecoach United Counties. When Stagecoach took over Cambus, Huntingdon went with the realignment. In 1999 Stagecoach United Counties became Stagecoach East.

This book is designed to complement the *History of United Counties* in 17 volumes by Mr Roger Warwick MCIT, and I am very grateful to Roger for all his help with preparing this compilation.

These two volumes include memories by about 150 of the staff, including past and present officials, engineers and fitters, inspectors, drivers, conductors, conductresses, union representatives, administrative staff, and retired staff, some of whom are still working in a part-time capacity.

Some of the interviews are with non-staff members, people who used the buses, had relatives who worked for the company, or were bus enthusiasts who knew the general picture behind the company.

A picture that sums up the family that was the bus company. One of the longest-serving employees, top engineer Jim Foreman, from the Central Works Training Unit, presents an award to one of the youngest, Neil Wilmin, star apprentice in 1988. See Chapter 2 for their memories. *Northampton Chronicle and Echo*

This aerial photograph, taken on 27 July 1966, shows the United Counties complex in Bedford Road, Northampton. In the bottom left-hand corner is Midsummer Meadow, and above that to the left is Beckets Park. Top middle is Northampton General Hospital, with the orchard coming down to the back of the Works. The Head Office building is next to Northampton Depot, with the Central Works behind. *Northampton Chronicle and Echo*

1
Northampton Head Office

When United Counties moved to Northampton from Irthlingborough, the headquarters and main works were situated together in Bedford Road. These buildings were closed and sold in 1990, making way for an apartment development. The Head Office and works were then split up: the main works were at Bedford, but the Head Office

The only full photograph of the staff at Bedford Road Head Office is this one taken outside the front of the building in 1964.

Back row: W. Stainton, Jack Hartley, J. Collins, Derek Merry, George Theobald, Sid Wesley, Bernard Routham, Bob Coote, Peter Brooksbank, Bob Whiteley, Les Bidewell, Les King, George Darlow, Leonard Gentle.

Middle row: Stan Simons, Peter Minney, Tom White, George Hawkins, Bert Seaman, Frank Gatehouse, Bob Rumbold, Maurice Jewitt, Rance Muscutt, Neville Ayres, Ray Goldstraw, Howard 'Johnny' Johnson, Roger Warwick.

Front row: Ralph Arnold, Peter Warhurst, 'Pop' Mayo, Hans 'Tich' Hawes, Doug Neale, Peter York, Harold Allchin, Madge Halton, John McRobert, Frank Ward, Percy Greaves, Reg Mitchell, John Buckby.

Seated: Fred Merriman, Rethe Cherry, John Robinson (General Manager), Ken Wellman, George Sell. *R. J. Butler collection*

remained in Northampton
at Rothersthorpe Avenue,
with a reduced staff, a small
engineering workshop and bus
storage area.

**General Manager Mr John
Wood and his wife (extreme left)
with the Mayor and Mayoress
of Bedford, Mr and Mrs Ken
Wellman, Stan Burton, Maurice
Jewitt and Dick Watson.**
*Bedfordshire Times, Dick Watson
collection*

**General Manager John
Robinson (extreme right) with
Maurice Jewitt, Dick Watson
and civic dignitaries at Bedford.**
Dick Watson collection

Miss Rethe Cherry

Miss Cherry worked for United
Counties as Personal Assistant to the
General Manager at the Head Office
in Bedford Road, Northampton.
She joined the company in 1945 at a
weekly rate of £2 3s 4d and retired in
1976. Her starting time was 9.00am
but Miss Cherry always was there
at 8.30am to open the post for the
managers.

During her working years Miss
Cherry worked with the following General Managers:
Reginald Pittard (1945-54), John Robinson (1954-
64), John Wood (1964-72), Edward ('Teddy') Dravers
(1972-75) and Colin Clubb (1975-76). Each had a
different way of doing his job and it took time for
Miss Cherry to discover their individual methods.
Some wanted everything done yesterday and others
were considerate and only pushed
when the work was genuinely needed
in a hurry. Miss Cherry was also
responsible for the stationery and
office equipment replacement and
maintenance. At times she would
have to go out to depots to audit the

stocks.

In one manager's case she also watched over his
Labrador, 'Laddy'. The dog was very good most of the
time. However, one persistent representative was sent
packing when 'Laddy' was guarding the office and bit
him.

Over the 31 years that Miss Cherry worked at
Bedford Road the offices changed, with the corridor

**Miss Cherry's office (left) with
the cherry tree and the back of
the remaining house in Vigo
Terrace.** *Roger Warwick collection*

being added in the 1960s and teams moving and changing size as needed. The General Manager's office and Miss Cherry's office had windows at the back of the building, on the ground floor. The Traffic Manager, Assistant Traffic Manager and Traffic Office were also on the ground floor.

Visitors using the front door were received by the receptionist/ telephonist. However, those in the know used to bypass this area and come in through the garage door, a practice that was frowned upon.

The top-floor offices included those of the Company Secretary,

Fred Merriman retired as Company Secretary in March 1975. He received his gift from Colin Clubb. *Colin Clubb collection*

One of the annual awards ceremonies; those pictured include Dennis Allen, Stanley Armstrong, Des Banyard, Frances Piercy, Alan Buttiphant, Lou Chapman, Peggy Jarrett, Ted Vickery and Norman Redhead. *Northampton Chronicle and Echo*

Mr Merriman, then Mr Frank Phillips, Assistant Company Secretary Victor Brown, then Roger Wigmore, Chief Engineer Eric Tuff and Assistant Engineer Mr Smith.

There were also offices for the secretary to the Company Secretary and other secretarial offices. Miss Frances Piercy also had her Waybill Office upstairs. At one time Miss Piercy employed up to 100 full- and part-time staff, who processed every waybill produced by conductors and, later, drivers. Some of these staff worked at home.

The Board Room was above the General Manager's office, and Miss Cherry spent much of her time attending meetings in this room.

At times of looming strikes Miss Cherry was very busy, accompanying the General Manager to numerous meetings, providing moral as well as administrative support. In some cases she was working so many hours that the General Manager's wife kept a spare bed for her, so she could work on and get in early the next day. At busy times she worked up to 60 hours a week to make sure the job was done to her exacting standards. During the National Bus Strike

Miss Cherry was given a lift to Northampton; when the staff at Wellingborough heard about this she was met when the car arrived, and they threatened to turn it over if she used it.

Miss Cherry had many dealings with other personal assistants and secretaries, not only at Northampton but at all the depots. As General Manager's Personal Assistant she gained respect from all her colleagues and in most cases they made sure her requests were given top priority.

In earlier years Miss Cherry's and the General Manager's offices overlooked the back gardens of Vigo Terrace, also the property of the bus company. However, as the works grew larger these properties were nearly all knocked down; a bungalow, where Mr Merriman lived, and one house remained. Others were used as stores or training schools before being knocked down to make way for bus parking.

When Miss Cherry started, United Counties served Northamptonshire with a few services into neighbouring counties. After the amalgamation with the Western Division of Eastern National and later Luton Corporation, the company had about 2,000

A long-service awards dinner in 1975, including, in the back row, R. Whitmore, Fred Campion, Des Banyard and Eric Brown; in the middle row, Reg Moule, Joe Keech, Alan Buttiphant and Colin Clubb; and in the front row D. G. F. Rawlinson, Peggy Jarrett, Len Waller and Mrs Madge Halton. Those honoured were J. Ashelford, H. Smith, R. Whitmore, Miss B. Barnard, R. W. Barnard, A. Berry, J. Gibson, B. Gudgin, L. Humberstone, J. Keech, P. Kelly, S. Lilford, Miss E. Panting, H. Pulley, E. Sorrell, G. Scholes, W. Warren, V. Watson, D. Wicks and P. Walker. *Colin Clubb collection*

employees. The number varied over the years as required by the passenger numbers.

Many of the staff from Northampton went to work by company scheduled services. In Miss Cherry's case this was on the Irthlingborough to Northampton service, while other colleagues would be travelling from Burton Latimer, Finedon and Wellingborough. The bus driver would slow right down at the bottom of Cheyne Walk and all Bedford Road staff would alight. At her interview, Miss Cherry was told that she would be given a bus pass, supposedly worth 10 shillings a week.

Miss Cherry did not drive when she started at Northampton. On hearing this, the Driving Instructor, Mr Chambers, decided that she should learn, and taught her himself.

Miss Rethe Cherry receives a long-service award from Guy Newberry. *Steve Loveridge collection*

Lunch was taken in the Café at Derngate Bus Station. Shepherd's pie and chips with a cup of tea was 1s 3d; this was not subsidised. The Café manageress was Madge Halton. Derngate was a good bus station but unfortunately the new one at Greyfriars was not so

friendly and Miss Cherry walked from Abington Square to Bedford Road, as it was nearer.

Miss Cherry used to arrange the Annual Company Dinner. This was held in a local hotel and was attended by managers, their partners and invited guests. Awards were given out at some of these events.

When she retired, Miss Cherry was given a painting by one of her

Miss Cherry pictured on her retirement in 1976 with the painting and other gifts. *NBC News*

colleagues, depicting the offices and a cherry tree outside. This is one of her most valued leaving presents and has pride of place on her wall.

Edward (Teddy) Dravers

Edward Dravers began his career in the bus industry in 1937 as a traffic trainee at the Ribble Headquarters in Preston. Although named Edward, he was more usually known as Teddy.

In the war years, 1939-45, Teddy was sent to the Company's Northern Area, based at Carlisle, with sub-depots at Penrith, Keswick and Ambleside. It was during the Dunkirk evacuation that heavy transport problems arose. This involved rail transport throughout the country, and buses were provided from the railheads to various army camps in the area. Ribble became very involved in this task.

Teddy was later drafted to Liverpool as Assistant to the Area Superintendent, to assist with the organisation of the services following severe air raids on the area and to aid in boosting the morale of the staff.

In due course he became the company's Southern Area Superintendent and from there went on to various companies including East Midland and Southdown,

before going to United Counties in 1972 as General Manager, a post vacated by the retirement of John Wood after 47 years in the Industry. The Eastern Counties General Manager and National Bus Company Eastern Area Group Manager in 1973 was Mr W. T. Skinner, who was next above the General Manager of United Counties and would have been his main contact with Head Office in London.

Teddy found this an interesting move, as his main bus industry background was with the BET group of companies, whereas United Counties was a Tilling company. These two groups were merged with the formation of the National Bus Company (NBC). However, he found that bus operations were ultimately the same whichever bus company you worked for, and he had to solve some of the same problems that prevailed.

Fleet maintenance was the greatest immediate concern. Any emergencies at outlying depots seemed

A Bedford Gala Dinner with (back row, l-r) Stan Burton, Jack Hartley, Maurice Jewitt, George Walden and Dick Watson, and (front row) John Birks, Edward Dravers and Howard 'Johnny' Johnson. *Dick Watson collection*

to involve senior engineers rushing off to deal with them to the detriment of the fleet control tasks they usually performed. This situation was exacerbated by the take-over of Luton Corporation buses following that company's acceptance of being nationalised and United Counties having to take over a fleet of somewhat run-down vehicles.

To cope with the Luton problems, it was agreed that the company should create two new posts of Area Engineer, one based at Kettering and the other in Luton. This allowed the maintenance staff at Headquarters to concentrate on the fleet overhaul programme without any further hindrance.

Teddy also persuaded the NBC to allow the purchase of some lightweight Bedford single-deckers to work the rural routes and thus allow the heavier vehicles to work the urban routes.

At a later date there was a further collapse, of Court Line Coaches, a company that served Luton and Luton Airport from districts south of the town. Unfortunately this take-over also incurred more maintenance problems.

A challenging project was the development, construction and growth of Milton Keynes. At that time it was still in the process of creation, and necessitated many meetings with the Development Corporation officials, with requirements for the development of extra services. However, Teddy left United Counties before this project was completed.

The provision of bus services and their standard of efficiency were often subject of criticism by local Members of Parliament. Many were of the opinion that they had a degree of control over bus companies now that they were nationalised. For this reason, United Counties invited its local MPs to Northampton Head Office to be shown how the company worked and the problems being experienced. The MP for Wellingborough, Peter Fry, and the MP for South Bedfordshire soon became good allies for the company, but no progress could be made with the two MPs for Luton. One became so hostile that he raised questions in the House of Commons concerning the standard of service in his area and the ability of the management. However, the Minister, who was supported by the MP for South Bedfordshire, rebuffed his endeavours.

The senior management of United Counties included John Birks as Traffic Manager, who soon went on to become Traffic Manager at Midland Red, being replaced by Brian Horner. The Chief Engineer, Mr Sell, retired and was replaced by Mike Carr. They soon settled in and helped to sort out the many problems. There were worries with the Accountants Department, which was well established in its methods and needed updating. The General Manager's Secretary, Miss Rethe Cherry, proved invaluable to Teddy and helped him greatly while the company went through this difficult period, which was much appreciated.

On the union side, regular meetings were held with staff representatives at depot, regional and national levels. The local regional representative was George Walden, who was very helpful in smoothing over any problems that arose.

During his time at Southdown, Teddy had worked very closely with the Chief Engineer, Colin Clubb, who had subsequently moved on as General Manager at Yorkshire Traction. Knowing that the chief problems at United Counties continued to be on the engineering side, Teddy put forward Colin's name to replace him, due to his engineering background; the approach was accepted and Colin thus moved to Northampton.

Teddy left United Counties in January 1975 to become General Manager of the Crosville Bus Company. Crosville had 1,000-plus buses at that time and was the largest company in the group.

After Crosville, Teddy worked as an executive at the National Travel coaching business before retiring to Sussex in 1980. During this job Edward was very impressed with the organisation of the main hubs at Cheltenham, Victoria Coach Station and Sheffield. One thing from this time that affected United Counties and all other bus companies with express routes was the centralising of the organisation of these services. The vehicles were all painted white with a corporate logo, as National Express. This name still exists, but under private management rather than nationalised control. Services were renumbered to a national rather than local regime, and extended tours were also reorganised at this time.

Colin and Judith Clubb

Colin graduated in Mechanical Engineering in 1957 and, after a short Student Engineering Apprenticeship at AEC Southall, he joined the bus industry as a Technical Assistant at Devon General, Torquay, in 1958. He moved with his wife Judith to Newcastle-upon-Tyne to work as Technical Assistant at Northern General in 1960, followed by a move to The North Western Road Car Co as Assistant Engineer in 1962.

In 1965 he moved again with his family to Aldershot to take up the position of Chief Engineer at the Aldershot & District Traction Co, and in late 1968 took up a similar position at Southdown Motor Services.

In 1973 Colin was appointed General Manager of the Yorkshire Traction Company in Barnsley, but in early 1975 he moved again to Northampton to take up the post of General Manager at United Counties. Colin describes this as a friendly family business, and he and Judith settled well into the life of Northampton and still live there to this day.

As experienced with previous companies, Colin felt at home straight away and appreciated the way the staff at Northampton welcomed him into the team. He recalls that throughout his time at United Counties he would pay visits to various depots, sometimes

A photograph taken at one of the company dinners: from left to right, the couples are Peter and Janet Brundle, John and Pauline Buckby, Frank and Olive Phillips, Colin and Judith Clubb, Mike and Heather Carr, and Jack and Edith Hartley. *Colin and Judith Clubb collection*

unannounced, and would endeavour to meet and talk with as many of the staff as possible. He felt that this was an essential part of building a team spirit and developing cohesion within the company. On occasions, depot problems were raised at central meetings by garage trade union representatives. One such concerned a problem at Luton Garage and the representative, Dennis Mulligan, mentioned this at a meeting in Northampton. Colin surprised everybody at Luton by going down to the garage to see the problem at first hand. In his own words, Dennis

The 'bus push' people, including Colin Clubb (centre) and Freddy and Mrs Wood (right). *Colin and Judith Clubb collection*

was very impressed with the way that the General Manager was happy to become involved practically to get the buses back on the road.

As a manager, Colin gained great respect from his staff for this and the other ways he treated them. Even when he had to make harsh decisions, he was respected and the trade unions treated him as an equal and not as an opponent.

Both Judith and Colin enjoyed the social side and regularly attended events all over the company. One such event, Colin recalls, was joining in with other staff members to push a bus a number of times round the perimeter of a lake at Billing Aquadrome. This event was most successful, raising £1,500 worth of valuable funds for charities. The Chairman of NBC at that time, Mr F. Wood, came up from London with his wife to be present at the event.

Colin says that he was fortunate in having an experienced and well-respected team at United Counties. His Personal Secretary was Miss Rethe Cherry, who was also respected by all who came in contact with her, for she had worked with many General Managers and Chief Officers and had a vast knowledge of the company going back over many years.

When Colin joined United Counties in 1975, he found the company actively engaged with Milton Keynes Development Corporation in the provision of transport services for the new town of Milton Keynes. This was a unique and most interesting period in the history of the company, in so far as it was closely involved with the Corporation in the design and progressive introduction of these services and attendant facilities ahead of population growth.

A further interesting project Colin remembers commenced in 1978/79 when proposals were put forward by the Local Authority at Northampton for development of the Derngate and Greyfriars sites. Derngate Bus Station had been in use for nearly 40 years and was a well-used and well-known facility in the town. The Borough Council wished to acquire the site for building a new theatre complex and at the same time was proposing to redevelop the Greyfriars area, part of which would include a new bus and coach terminus. This new facility opened in 1976 and the theatre in the 1980s.

In 1979 Colin moved to the Midland Red Company in Birmingham as General Manager, transferring to London Country Bus in 1981 as Managing Director. Following the division of London Country Bus into separate operating companies and privatisation in 1987/88, he moved once more, this time to London Transport to head up London Northern, one of the many new companies formed from the division of London Transport Buses. He remained there until March 1993, when he retired to live full-time in Northampton with Judith.

John Tate

After university John Tate became a Management Trainee with the National Bus Company. After working for the Yorkshire Traction Bus Company, John became the Traffic Manager for United Counties on 1 May 1976, then in February 1979 he became the second-youngest General Manager and Director of an NBC company. He remained at United Counties until 1987, when Stagecoach took over. Coming from a busy coal-mining and factory area to the rural Midlands was quite an eye-opener for John. He has since got to know the area well and still lives locally by choice.

He recalls that on his first day he was taken out to lunch at Hardingstone. On the way a United Counties bus passed with six passengers aboard. John asked if all the buses ran about with no passengers, and was told that six passengers was a good load for that service. This was strange, as the local buses in Yorkshire were heaving with customers and were being duplicated all the time.

John remembers that the Area Traffic Manager South was Bob Rumbold and North was Leonard Gentle. John particularly remembers the trip round the Northern area with Mr Gentle, whose driving was unusual and very interesting.

Others remembered were Bob White, Brian McCall, Barry Warner (Chief Engineer North) and Des Banyard (union man at Wellingborough), especially as John had to close a depot and Wellingborough closed in 1986. Others he remembered were Dennis Ord and Jeff Gundell.

The closure of Wellingborough Depot caused much bad feeling, and was due to a reduction in the number of vehicles needed. In 1978 Northampton County Council had withdrawn funding for routes worth £600,000, which caused the problem; one depot had to go and Wellingborough was the one. In 1983 John had to deal with many industrial disputes, but all were resolved.

John remembers that his team was instrumental in negotiating favourable working procedures with the rival Northampton Corporation Transport. Previously United Counties had not been allowed to pick up or drop off within the town boundary. In later years some services covered the Duston area, but after talks the services to East Northampton areas around Weston Favell started.

John enjoyed a good 'bus war'. He had a small battle with Yorks Bros at Cogenhoe and, later in his career, with Fenland Travel while working for Viscount Buses in Peterborough. Both were successful.

One event that John remembers were the negotiations with Milton Keynes Corporation for a depot at Winterhill. The solicitors worked a marathon 36 hours to thrash out the deal for rent.

Milton Keynes was unusual in being a grid city, with roads running north-south and east-

Market Analysis
Project
Mobile Office

The MAP team with their Bristol FS 705 outside Greyfriars Bus Station.
Steve Loveridge collection

west. Providing bus services was a nightmare as the population would not walk to the bus stops on these routes. In later years services called in to most housing estates.

John thinks that the closure of United Counties Engineering was appalling; it was a decision made outside the company and he had no control over it.

Market Analysis Project (MAP) was a Conservative Government initiative to find out what services were required by the population. A team was set up at No 3 Albion Place and the findings were reported back to the Board. As a result, many revisions were made and routes became extended or shortened as required, and many vehicles and staff were saved as a result, while those remaining worked more efficiently. John felt this was a good initiative.

The main revision of Milton Keynes services occurred in 1978. At the same time Rushden Depot was closed, with most staff transferring to Wellingborough. Rushden Depot was too small to expand, whereas Wellingborough had all the land behind. John regretted this action as all the staff were 'great people'.

Ben Colson joined the company in 1984 and was responsible for many initiatives that came out of MAP. Included in these were Corby's 'Magic Minis'. John

was very supportive of Ben and is particularly proud of the Coachlinks services they set in motion. The 'mini bus' phenomenon was created by a director of the National Bus Company and United Counties used it to order lots of minibuses.

In Corby the 'Magic Minis' were one of the many initiatives to take market share from the local taxis, driven mainly by moonlighting steel-workers. In later years former London Transport Routemasters were used. In John's opinion, these initiatives helped but did not solve the issue completely.

The other Corby initiative, which did not happen, was the giant new theme park 'Wonderworld', designed to give employment to ex-steelworkers after the plant closure. In John's opinion this was a couple of advertising men and an advertising hoarding and nothing else.

In the 1980s John was Chair of the Board for London Crusader, an initiative to promote sightseeing services in London. Others on the board were Bernard Davis and Mike Vigor. By canvassing hotel porters, recommendations were made that resulted in very good passenger figures.

John was instrumental in the conversion of buses from crewed vehicles (driver and conductor), to one-man-only (OMO) driver-only vehicles. This

involved many negotiations with
the unions. Some depots were easy
to convert, while others were more
difficult. United Counties bought
many Bristol VR double-deckers and
Bristol RELL single-deckers for this
exercise. Wellingborough had only
one Bristol VR double-decker, and
that remained crewed for a long time,
due to union resistance to OMO.

In 1981 John was instrumental
in producing 'The Way Ahead',
a document for change. In 1985

Ian Stewart MP, John Tate and
Michael Morris MP discuss bus
matters. *Northampton Chronicle
and Echo*

he was instructed to split the
company into three. This created a smaller United
Counties (Bedford, Biggleswade, Corby, Kettering,
Northampton and Huntingdon – Huntingdon later
became part of Cambus), Milton Keynes became a
company, and the Southern area became Luton &
District.

John was part of the unsuccessful proposed buy-
out team for United Counties in 1986. His job also
involved showing the company to other proposed
purchasers, Stagecoach's Brian Souter being one of
them. Brian's team was eventually the successful new
owner. At the time of the take-over, John particularly
remembers that the union team in Bedford were very
opposed to the sale.

John is a member of FELIX, an organisation for
former managers of the National Bus Company, which
provides opportunities to meet up with old colleagues
and put the world to rights. Earlier it had been used as
a networking exercise.

John only went to NBC head office occasionally;
most of his NBC meetings were held with Area
Directors at their place of work. He remembers one of
these directors well, Derrick Fytche. These meetings
were useful when things were needed in a hurry. One
year six new coaches were needed urgently and, as a
result of a regional meeting, they duly arrived quickly
and the services started.

One perk of the General Manager's job in those
days was a company car and chauffeur. United
Counties Engineering was just fitting air-conditioning
to United Counties' and other coaches, and John
thought it would be a good marketing tool to say that
the GM had it in his car, which was duly done; this car
was the only one to be fitted at that time.

Another initiative was sponsorship of the arts. This
entailed sponsoring ballets and concerts, and United

Counties had the advantage of supplying Executive
Coaches 81-83 for patrons of these events; these
were usually business people and thus would become
customers for their corporate events. The launch was
at the old Bus Station at Derngate, now the Royal &
Derngate theatre complex, including a bus done up
with sponsorship of the company. These coaches were
also available for private hire. John was a member of
Northampton Rotary, which expected a free coach for
all its requirements. This did not happen.

Unfortunately, John was not able to get to know
all his staff – there were too many of them, especially
at Luton, and getting them together was impractical
while still keeping a service running.

One part of the General Manager's post that
was rarely talked about were visits to the House of
Commons, in order to lobby local MPs and to deal
with any queries that they had. MPs like quiet lives,
and if the GM would solve the problems of their
constituents they were welcomed with open arms.

John used to attend the company award
ceremonies and would give out awards. This bit he
enjoyed, but he did not like the venues; due to the size
of the events, they were held in 'impersonal' rooms in
'impersonal' hotels.

Stagecoach's Brian Souter offered John a job, but
he declined and left in 1987 to work at Viscount in
Peterborough. By 2007 John was a part-time director
of Kettering Hospital and a director of the probation
service.

Brian Horner

Brian joined the bus industry in 1955 as a company
trainee at Cumberland Motor Services, and over the
next five years trained in every department of the
business, including driving and conducting buses,

and bus maintenance. After a short time acting as Depot Superintendent at Millom, he moved to the United Automobile Company in 1960 as Assistant Area Traffic Superintendent in the Durham area. He moved to Darlington Head Office in 1961 to deal with operating licensing, preparing applications for services and fare changes or variations.

In 1962 Brian was appointed as Assistant Traffic Manager at Southern Vectis on the Isle of Wight, and had great experience in operating very high-frequency services. This was due to holidaymakers doubling the population in the summer, and the company having a successful tours and excursion business.

In 1966 Brian was appointed as Traffic Manager for United Welsh at Swansea, his main task being to amalgamate that company with the South Wales Transport Company, Neath and Cardiff Luxury Coaches, and Thomas Bros of Port Talbot. This needed to happen with the formation of the National Bus Company, itself an amalgamation of the Tilling and BET groups. Included in the new company was most of the Western Area of Western Welsh Company. As a result of the new company, known as the South Wales Transport Company, 200 vehicles were saved.

In 1973 Brian was appointed a Traffic Manager at United Counties. He was based at the Head Office at Northampton and was responsible for the operations, service development and union negotiation. There were four traffic areas, Northampton, Kettering, Bedford and Luton, each with a Superintendent who reported to the Traffic Manager.

Brian had two able Assistant Traffic Managers. One was Jack Hartley, who had been with the company for many years and had a great deal of background knowledge. The other was Peter Brundle, who was very strong on service planning and development. Brian coordinated work with the Area Offices under Bob Rumbold at Luton, Maurice Jewitt at Bedford, Len Gentle at Kettering, and Norman Maycock at Northampton.

The company had to deal with the London Overspill, which resulted in New Town development at Corby, Milton Keynes, Northampton, Wellingborough and Luton; the latter included Dunstable, Houghton Regis and parts of Hertfordshire in the Hitchin area. This work brought about difficult union negotiations, especially at Luton, where there were two branches to deal with as a result of the take-over of the Luton Corporation Transport bus operation. Differential wage structures and government wage constraints made the situation more complex and often caused disputes and strikes.

Brian enjoyed the strong support of his two General Managers, first Teddy Dravers and later Colin Clubb, who successfully guided the company through many hard times. One of these difficulties was that United Counties had an old fleet and a severe shortage of vehicles due to all the service expansion.

A Stony Stratford dinner with, from the left, Sid Major, Norman and Mrs Maycock, 'Johnny' and Mrs Johnson, Judith and Colin Clubb, Charlie and Mrs Thorne, and Linda and Brian Horner. *Colin Clubb collection*

This led to many engineering difficulties and the need for urgent workshop improvements and expansion. Many second-hand vehicles were brought in from other group companies and, as a short-term measure, some 50 Bedford and Ford Lightweight buses were purchased with Willowbrook and Duple bodies. Then a fairly rapid delivery of new Bristol VRs and Leyland Nationals arrived to replace the older and non-standard vehicles.

Brian has many memories of company union negotiations with the depots and the Central Committee. These were very ably chaired by General Managers, enabling the company to gradually return to a more settled organisation and making profits to meet its financial duty to the Government.

Brian pays his respects to the many staff and union representatives with whom he worked and negotiated. These included the late George Walden (TGWU District Organiser), Bill Morris, who later became General Secretary of the TGWU and was later knighted for his services, and local branch secretaries Dennis Mulligan, Eric Stock and Des Banyard.

During his stay at United Counties Brian was instrumental in building up good working relationships with his contemporaries in Northampton Corporation Transport. First was a Mr O'Donnell, who was not very forthcoming; he would visit Bedford Road annually but a return visit rarely happened. Brian went to see him about a joint approach to the new development of housing and industry in Weston Favell. This was a positive move and would have benefited both companies and the residents of the new area, but Mr O'Donnell would not be involved.

However, in 1974 Mr O'Donnell was replaced by Chris Mahony, with whom Brian got on well. Each would visit the other and tour their premises, exchanging ideas and cooperating well on new projects. Other ideas were exchanged, including picking up and setting down on common routes into town. Many of the historical restrictions were lifted during their time. Brian's belief in a common industry with differing interests and differing priorities seemed to be right, with the companies building on the strengths of each other and above all creating an atmosphere in which they could talk and, with Colin Clubb, move many ideas forward.

Brian decided to check out the opposition one Saturday morning and was seen in the town centre making notes. He watched the vehicles arriving, changing crews and leaving again. He was reported back at Northampton Transport and at Derngate. As a company official one was always in the forefront of action.

As the National Bus Company was being formed, with its new image, including the double 'N' logo, the United Counties General Manager called a special meeting to discuss the visit of the Chairman, Sir Frederick Wood, and Chief Executive, Jim Skyrme,

to see what progress had been made in showing the corporate image in United Counties. The General Manager addressed the chief officers thus: 'Come you in gentlemen, sit you down. Now gentlemen, I am perturbed as very little appears to have been done about this most important matter of corporate identity. Now I hope you will relieve my concern by making some positive reports.'

The Chief Engineer had made some progress. He had ordered five flags to be flown at the company's flagship depots of Bedford, Kettering, Luton and Northampton. The fifth flag was very important, as it would be flown at Bedford Road when the General Manager was in residence, just like the Queen at Buckingham Palace.

The General Manager was very impressed and passed on to Brian, who was considering his moves. The General Manager suggested a whole list of measures, which Brian would report back about in one week. The Company Secretary was keeping quiet and was told not to look smug, as he would have to pay for the exercise.

This General Manager was being mimicked by his junior officers. He called them in one day and told them that they should stamp it out. They were never sure whether he had heard them, knew who it was, or had just guessed. Suffice to say that, his impression was never heard again.

Brian also had a good understanding with local independent operators, such as York Bros, Wesley Coaches and Brittons Coaches. Mr Britton was a former employee of United Counties and was known affectionately as the 'Ancient Britton', due to the age of his fleet.

Finally Brian feels that he humanised staff and industrial relations during his time at United Counties, and was able to extend that to Northampton Corporation Transport, as well as developing good relations with the county and district authorities.

Brian moved on in 1976 to be General Manager of East Yorkshire, based at Hull, and in 1978 moved to West Yorkshire as General Manager, retiring in 1987. He was then appointed as an Assistant Traffic Commissioner in 1988 and did this job until he fully retired in 2001. His principal work was presiding over Traffic Courts. These dealt with service registrations and driver and operating discipline, and included the same things for heavy goods operators, including environmental matters connected with operating centres.

Stan Simons

Stan Simons died on 20 November 2003, and his account of his days with United Counties is reproduced by permission of Mrs Simons and Mrs Glasspool.

Being the longest-serving employee of United Counties, with 48 years' service on my retirement in 1982, I thought it was about time to record some my reminiscences of the 'good old days'.

There were two elderly ladies living in Wellington Street, Kettering, who were milliners and made hats for the local well-to-do. At about 13 years of age on Saturday mornings I used to deliver these hats on my bicycle. For this I was paid the princely sum of threepence per hat. Quite often the grateful recipient gave me a tip, even as much as sixpence.

At the age of 15 I obtained a part-time job at the *Kettering Evening Telegraph*. I helped in the publishing department producing the *Leader and Guardian,* which came out once a week on a Friday. This always had a children's competition page, giving away quite nice prizes. I won a number of these until I was banned. Mr Bellamy was the Publisher and I had to be there at 6.00am, as the **Leader** started rolling off the press at that time. Saturday afternoons I was there again helping on the 'Pinkun', the sports paper with all the football results. I can still visualise the sub-editors and reporters laying on their desks and tables, telephones stuck to their ears.

During the summer school holidays of 1932 I obtained employment at a leather factory. This lasted a week, as I couldn't stand the smell of untreated leather. My Dad then got me a job in the clicking room of a large boot and shoe factory, leading to pattern-cutting. Again this only lasted about a week – it wasn't my cup of tea.

After the end of the holidays, and these episodes, I went back to school and no one was any the wiser. I then did another full year in the sixth form before leaving to obtain permanent employment.

Good jobs were not easy to find in those days and progressing to university for an ordinary middle-class lad almost unheard of. You had to have a family with money, and we had very little.

Eventually I obtained employment with Frosts Bus Company of Hawthorne Road, Kettering, working in the office as a general dogsbody. There was only one other gentleman in the office, and he also doubled up as a ticket inspector. My job consisted of checking the waybills and cash brought in by the conductors. Each ticket had a separate value and the conductor had a Bell Punch machine. When he sold a ticket this was removed from the rack he carried and a hole stamped in it from this little machine. The ticket inspector was essential, as it was easy to swindle the company. If the conductor had a friend on the bus he would give him a used ticket, or issue one of a lower denomination for the journey.

Two brothers, Harold and John, owned Frosts. Harold was the manager and John the engineer. They had quite a fleet of buses and coaches, among them Reos, Lancias, Leyland PLSC3 buses and Tiger coaches. They had the monopoly of the service from Kettering to Corby and this was developing rapidly. They even ran this service on Christmas Day.

Harold owned a Lancia car and in the summer he would sometimes take me with him and his wife to the seaside for a day's outing. On one occasion his wife went into the sea and got out of her depth; she couldn't swim. I went in and rescued her and forever afterwards Harold said I had saved her life and was eternally grateful.

At Frosts we had a Thornycroft bus with a Dorman Ricardo diesel engine and I actually had a go at driving this, out of service of course. This was the one and only time I drove a bus.

During 1933/36 United Counties Omnibus Co Ltd was busy buying up all the small operators and on 14 October 1934 it took over Frosts. I went to work in the Chief Engineer's office at Irthlingborough, which was then the Head Office and Main Workshops. My first Chief Engineer was Mr J. S. Gavin, who came to United Counties from being a ships' engineer; can you imagine such a qualification being accepted today to

A young Stan Simons. *Simons family collection*

fill the demanding role of Chief Engineer? His only administrative staff was a Chief Clerk and two youths – of which I was one. The offices were heated with coal fires and we would stack them up as far as possible. At that time the buses were being repainted from red, white and blue to green and cream. Now, as part of Stagecoach, they have reverted back to red, white and blue.

The first diesel bus they had was the aforementioned Thornycroft, which came with the Frosts purchase. Most buses were hand-cranked in those days – no starter motors. Many a driver sprained or even broke his wrist trying to start the engine.

In 1935 we had the famous drivers and conductors strike, which lasted for many weeks, as they did not consider that roughly a shilling an hour was enough to live on for a 48-hour week. On reflection, can you blame them? They were also dismissed in those days for such things as being too expensive on gearboxes or talking to passengers while driving. The 48-hour-rota men were the crème de la crème; there was also a 32-hour rota and casual labour queuing up each day for a day's work.

During the strike we had squads of policemen lining up each morning in the garage for inspection. Eight brand-new Leyland TD4 double-deckers were delivered and Mr Gavin, in his wisdom, decided to operate them with 'scab' labour. On return from service most of the windows had been broken and the tyres deflated by having the valves cut off. The panels were damaged to such an extent that they looked ready for the scrap heap. Fuel tank caps were also missing, where the strikers had tried to set light to the fuel by dropping matches in. Lucky for them diesel does not ignite very easily. To add insult to injury, we had a claim from an irate householder in Rushden claiming damages for his rockery, which had disappeared.

Then living in Kettering, I scrounged lifts or cycled to work each day, always calling in to the strike picket tent for a cup of tea before reporting for duty. I recall going home with a bodybuilder one evening in a small Morris van loaded with glass for Kettering depot. By the time we arrived most of the glass was broken with the bumping it had received.

I also remember standing in a shop doorway on a Sunday afternoon with some of the strikers. They all had a piece of brick or stones in their hands. Along came a police car, followed by a double-decker bus with wire netting over the windows, barbed wire around the autovac and tyre valves. After them came another police car, so the strikers decided discretion was the better part of valour and left the 'procession' alone. There was not a single passenger on the bus.

With great public support, collecting tins being prevalent, questions asked in the House of Commons and a special Traffic Commissioners' inquiry, this strike was particularly successful. Another took place the following year but this was a flop as there was no public support.

United Counties progressed until the outbreak of the Second World War with about 250 vehicles. Prior to the war I was Purchasing Officer, and as such in a reserved occupation. The winter of 1939/40 was dreadful with loads of snow and ice. One day I and my friend Pat Partridge, later superintendent of Stony Stratford Depot, tried to get home in freezing fog. I walked in front of the bus with a torch, while Pat sat on the wing shouting instructions to the driver. When we reached the bus stop in Earls Barton the bus kept sliding down the hill and finished up on the other side of the road. We eventually got to Finedon, where Pat lived, but could go no further. I and another friend, Norman Miller, slipping and sliding on the ice, managed to reach Burton Latimer. My girlfriend, Mary Ashby, lived in Burton, so I knocked on her door, but by then it was getting pretty late. She answered it, in her nightdress, and it was then that I thought it was about time I asked for her hand in marriage. We had been engaged for three or four years, having 'walked out' for about five years altogether.

Norman Miller joined the RAF and became a Spitfire pilot. Unfortunately he crashed and was killed. They gave him a full military funeral, and he is buried in Burton Latimer churchyard. He was an only child and his parents grieved for him until the end of their lives. Nothing in his bedroom was moved, only to clean. They turned to spiritualism for solace.

After this dreadful winter the Company Secretary, Mr Norman Rolfe, said he had to apply for a further six months' extension to my reservation. I told him not to bother as I would rather join the forces than go through the same again.

After that terrible winter of 1939/40 I went to Northampton Recruiting Office and volunteered to receive the King's shilling. Given the 'full monty' by the medical officer, I was graded B3, because of my bad eyesight. I asked to join the RAF but was told that the only position available was as a cook. I found out later that this wasn't true, as a friend of mine took up this offer but was never made a cook. It was just a ploy to get you to join the Army. On 4 September 1940 I joined the Royal Army Pay Corps as a private soldier, and was posted to the Pay Office at Leicester. I was there for quite some time and found accommodation for Mary and myself

As I was due to leave the Army they tried to persuade me to join up as a regular, but I declined. I wondered for a long time afterwards if I did right by going back to United Counties. I was also asked if I wished to become a schoolteacher. I suppose they were short of male teachers after the war. Demobbed in June 1946, with an exemplary character reference, I went back to United Counties, starting at £5 12s 6p per week after getting about £9 a week, with pay and allowances, in the Army. Someone else was in my old job, so I spent nearly a year in the Wages Office, where Frank Ward was the Chief Wages Officer.

Mary, my wife, had obtained the cottage at Burton Latimer while I was still in the Army and settled in with our eldest daughter, Diana.

On my return I was told one interesting little story. Apparently United Counties had Home Guard and Firewatching Sections. Mr Eric Tuff, Chief Engineer, and Mr Norman Rolfe, Company Secretary, were firewatching in the Traffic Office, sleeping on camp beds. Mr Rolfe, so I'm told, did not wear pyjamas but a long nightshirt. Nature calling, he had to go upstairs in the middle of the night. On his return he woke Mr Tuff who, seeing this apparition, nearly passed out, his hair literally standing on end. He always did believe in ghosts.

There is also a story of earlier in the war when Mr Gavin was Commander of the United Counties Home Guard Unit, going on exercise with his men. Crawling through undergrowth he suddenly stood up, shouted 'Charge!' and immediately tripped over a bramble into a muddy ditch.

To illustrate the accuracy of bus timings at that time, when I was courting I used to catch the 5 minutes past midnight bus on Saturday nights, running down the street at the last minute to do so. For three consecutive Saturdays running I missed it and walked the 4 miles home with a friend who had done the same. On the last occasion it poured with rain all the way, so on the Monday I made enquiries at the Traffic Department to find that the timing had changed to 3 minutes passed midnight. For the sake of 2 minutes we never saw the bus three times running.

On the journey home from work the scheduling boys were very good, and as I had to make a change at Finedon they worked it so that there was a bus waiting for me when I arrived. Nevertheless it was not uncommon for me to sleep through Finedon and finish up in Irthlingborough, the opposite direction from which I wished to go.

During the war, and for a year or two afterwards, all buses carried a full load and queues formed all over Derngate Bus Station; at Bay 1, the Wellingborough bay, queues even went out into the street. Company staff were given priority and, by showing their passes, could jump the queue, which was very nice for us, but the paying passengers were not very amused. If only we could get full loads like that today.

In January 1947 we had the worst snow blizzard since 1894, and it was virtually impossible to get out

of Burton Latimer, where we were living. I managed to struggle through to Burton railway station; there was no sign of life, but down the track I could see a train, about half a mile away. After a time it started moving and eventually the engine pulled up alongside me. It was a 'Royal Scot', a huge locomotive. The driver looked down at me and said, 'Where are you going, mate?' I replied that I wanted to get to Northampton. He said, 'Hop in, I'm going to Wellingborough but you'll have to get out there.' The train was going to Bedford, Luton and St Pancras. He pulled along the track and I got in one of the carriages.

I then walked, through the snow, to Wellingborough Depot, but of course the town was totally snowed in. At last one of our single-decker buses arrived, followed by a Morris Minor driven by Frank Chambers, the Chief Driving Instructor. They were loaded with drivers and conductors, all with spades and shovels. They had managed to dig their way through, so I went back with them. I have never seen anything like it: in some places the snow went over the top of the trees, about 16 feet high. These staff were the first to break through to the Northampton Road and Frank took me into work. I had to stay with Frank Ward, Chief Wages Clerk, and his wife in Northampton for the next three days, as it was impossible to get home.

One day in 1949 I stood waiting for the early morning bus at Burton Latimer and it never turned up. News then came through of an accident in Polewell Lane, Barton Seagrave, which transpired to be probably the worst accident in the history of United Counties. It was a very foggy morning and two double-deckers, one a Leyland TD2 and the other a Bristol K Type, collided, ripping a side completely out of each bus. There were a large number of passengers injured, some very seriously. The Leyland had its body taken off and was made into a breakdown lorry, while the K Type was repaired.

John Wood was the Chief Engineer during some of the war years and he later came back as our General

Luton in 1958, with Rethe Cherry, Charles Blomfield, Mary Simons and Frank Gatehouse.
Simons family collection

Manager. Eric Tuff followed him, being one of three brothers, all Chief Engineers in the bus industry. He finally retired as Chief Engineer of Midland Red.

One of the great characters at United Counties was the Works Superintendent, Sid Wesley. He couldn't say a sentence without using a swear word, but no one took any notice. He was always apologising to the office girls for his language. One of my jobs was preparing the minutes for Regional Chief Engineers' meetings. On one occasion a great argument arose between the Chief Engineers present on the torque required for tightening Gardner engine cylinder foot studs. In the end the Chairman, Tom Skinner, later a Chief General Manager for the area, sent for Sid and asked him how tight he tightened the studs. Sid's reply is unprintable, but he just said two words – '**** tight' – and that was the end of the argument. I was instructed not to minute this.

1952 arrived with the transfer of the Midland Division of Eastern National to United Counties, with an extra 250 buses. This was a major operation as at that time there was only the Chief Engineer with no engineering assistants to help, other than the likes of me. Charles Blomfield, Assistant Engineer at Eastern National, became our Chief and Frank Gatehouse Senior our first Assistant Engineer.

Frank was another great character, always willing to give everyone a helping hand. He did not care what he did if it got the job done – his specialty was erecting Essex bus-washing machines, and he would climb all over the girders in his efforts to get these installed.

On Friday evenings Charles Blomfield, Frank Gatehouse, Sid Wesley and myself used to go to the

Party time again with Mary Simons at the back and Rethe Cherry second from left at the front.
Simons family collection

Mary Simons, Frank Gatehouse, 'Johnny' Johnson, Mrs Johnson, Grace Neale and Dougy Neale.
Simons family collection

Drill Hall in Northampton to watch the wrestling. It was a ritual that we had four rounds of whiskies during these contests. One Friday, however, just before we were going, a message came through that a bus was in the River Lea at Luton, so we had to forget the wrestling and rush off to Luton.

The front of the bus was in the river and the back stuck on the embankment. Two breakdown lorries were needed to get it out. 'Johnny' Johnson, later to be Assistant Engineer, was in charge of one. Frank Gatehouse Junior went into the river up to his waist to shore up the bus so they could drag it out. We still had our whiskies – on the way home.

When Charles Blomfield retired he was succeeded by George Sell from Bristol. After him came Mike Carr, who had previously been with us as a Technical Assistant and left to become the Chief Engineer of the China Bus Company in Hong Kong. All in all I served under eight Chief Engineers, doing a variety of jobs,

including being in charge of Northampton Depot for nine years.

During this time I was on 24-hour call seven days a week from the Police Control Centre for the M1 motorway, for coaches breaking down. Many a time I had to fetch out Jack Hobbs, now Depot Engineer, in the middle of the night – but that is another story.

My main hobby for many years was keeping and breeding tropical fish. At Burton Latimer I had four tanks, two on each side of the fireplace. When we moved to Northampton I built a fish house in the garden, mostly from old panels from United Counties buses. It had no side windows, and all the natural light came from glass in the roof. Our house in Victoria Road was also painted in United Counties green, and it was said that when you pressed the bell the house would take off down the street! My compost heap has panels around it with the words 'United Counties' still emblazoned on them.

Mary Simons recalls that the house the family occupied in Brackley Road, Northampton, was owned by United Counties and built for the company by H. C. Janes Ltd of Luton for £2,800 in 1964. The family lived there until Mary moved in 2006. The rent was paid originally to United Counties, then Stagecoach until she moved. Both companies asked the Simons to buy the house but Stan would not do this, preferring to rent instead.

Frank Ward, the company's Chief Wages Clerk who requested Stan work in his office, rented a flat with his wife Barbara above the Café at Derngate Bus Station. Mary also remembers that one of the cooks in the Café was Anne Bass, née Webb.

Similarly, living in a flat above the offices at the

Stan Simons on his retirement after 48 years with United Counties, enjoying his present, a reclining chair. *NBC News*

The house in Brackley Road, Northampton, built for the Simons family by H. C. Janes Ltd and paid for by United Counties. *Roger Warwick collection*

White House Bus Station, in Stony Stratford, were Pat and Diane Partridge. When Pat left Stony Stratford he went to work for Aston Martin Lagonda at Newport Pagnell. When he worked in Northampton he and Stan used to catch the same bus to work and used to play dominos.

She also remembers Norman Abbott, a Foreman and AUEW Senior Shop Steward. He also was the senior spokesperson for all unions in United Counties.

The Partridge family. *Simons family collection*

Robert Whiteley

I worked at Head Office of the company from January 1941 to January 1986 (apart from May 1943 to September 1947 when I was involved with National Service).

When I first joined United Counties in 1941 I soon noticed that some people were 'bus nuts' and some were not. I remained one of the latter. I should also point out that although I retired as Publicity Officer my remit never covered Public Relations.

My first memories are dealing with complaints and refunds on stage services. In the 1950s I was involved in issuing School Term tickets, and on the take-over of the Midland section of Eastern National I was taken to Chelmsford by Traffic Manager Reginald Howe to see how they dealt with the matter.

Soon after this I was moved to deal with the Express Services, involving timetable requests, complaints, refunds, timetable leaflet compilation, printing, and distribution to depots and agents. My duties also included the supply of copy for the Stage Timetable booklet to the printers. I believe at this time the printers were Index Publishers of Dunstable. Later all Stage Timetables were printed as separate service leaflets and we changed to a local printer, Xpres Printers Ltd of Northampton.

While involved with Express Services, I organised and accompanied several agents' trips on the Nottingham to London service, explaining where the different stops were. I also visited Derby for two or three days, interviewing prospective witnesses for the Alfreton-London service, applied for jointly with Trent.

During the 1970s and 1980s, as far as I can remember, my team consisted of an artist, two or three clerks and a van driver, who looked after leaflet deliveries and placed in position the roadside timetables (about 2,000 sites) that were produced in the office.

The copy for the in-house bi-monthly newspaper, *Bus News,* was collected by me together with any photos (taken, developed and printed by me) and sent off to NBC for printing. Perhaps I was not in any pictures because I took them.

I was a member of the Traffic Office and worked in later years with Roger Warwick and Steve Loveridge.

I stayed for 45 years because I always found the variety of work interesting.

Dennis Lloyd

Dennis was born in 1936 and went to Northampton Grammar School. As a boy he used to go with his friends to watch the buses coming in and out of Derngate Bus Station on a Saturday morning. His favourite buses were the Leylands, including the former National MPU series double-deckers.

Living in Duston, he always used to go into town, with his mother, on the lower deck of the Leylands. He can remember that United Counties had many Leyland Lions at the time, some of which were rebodied. More of his favourite Leylands were 524-526, in the NV 1043 series. These had been reconditioned and lasted a lot longer than the rest of the type. Dennis and his sister remember being taken into the Derngate Café for a treat.

In the early 1950s Dennis went down to Derngate one Saturday and saw what he thought was a Northampton Corporation bus in the bus station. It turned out to be JWT 712, one of the two Lodekka demonstrators, in a red and cream livery, similar to the Corporation buses. However, it was numbered 822 and was on hire from West Yorkshire buses. It was very impressive with a gleaming radiator surround and a full bumper at the front.

Another day he arrived at Derngate to see a similar-looking green bus parked over in the tyre bay. This turned out to be United Counties' first Lodekka, numbered 950, which in its early days spent much of its time on the 312 service to Brixworth and Pitsford.

When he left school he went to work for Frames Tours in Gold Street, Northampton. After a while he decided to change jobs and as a result of his previous job was appointed to the Traffic Office at the United Counties Head Office in Bedford Road in 1955. His first job was clerk in charge of the extended coach tours; three were to North Wales, the Scottish Islands and the English Lakes, and the fourth to Devon and Cornwall. The main coaches were 35-seater luxury tourers, with reclining seats and personal address systems, driven by Len Bull and Tommy Reed. The work involved taking the bookings, sending out the luggage labels and tickets, and producing a seating plan.

In those days Donald Crew was the Traffic Manager. Dennis also remembers Peter York and Mary Collins; Ollie, Mary's husband, worked in the Central Works. Fred Merriman was known affectionately as 'Puzzle' Merriman, due to his hair cut.

While at Bedford Road, Dennis had to visit the Central Works to collect stationery. He used these opportunities to have a good look round and see what was new. He remembers that 'Pop' Mayo always wore a white coat.

After a while Dennis changed jobs and went to run the Enquiry Office at Derngate Bus Station. He worked with Peggy Hawkins, Yvonne Copson and a lady called Eileen. He also remembers Jean and Roger Warwick from those days. He thinks that Bristol VR 950 was allocated to Northampton at the behest of Roger as a replacement for the original Lodekka 950, but is not sure whether this is true or not. He also worked with John Coleman. Dennis was younger than the ladies, and at quiet periods they used to practise ballet around the office, at the back of the counter.

Dennis was looking after the Express Services at this time. The main service was on the Nottingham to London corridor, and most coaches on this run were 41-seaters. The work involved charting the bookings, liaising with Jesse James upstairs, who organised the crews, and the engineering department, who organised the vehicles.

Loading sheets were issued two days before the date of travel, although bookings were taken up to the time of departure from any stop. These later bookings caused much friction. The drivers used to ring Dennis to say that their vehicles were 'over the top', meaning that they had too many passengers. The drivers were not allowed to negotiate with inspectors at places such as Leicester and Nottingham to book duplicate vehicles; all that had to be done through Northampton, which could cause a delay. At the two-days-before

stage Dennis might already have booked duplicates, and these might also be overflowing. The main coach would do the whole run but the duplicates might start at other points along the route and only be needed one way.

At the end of their run, the coach drivers, an elite bunch, used to bring in their confirmed booking sheets for checking. These included Ron Faulkner and Mick Harris (whose uniform was always immaculate). Ron had a favourite Leyland double-decker, FEV 175, and would take that out rather than his allotted vehicle if it was spare. He was sad when it left the company.

Dennis worked for the Superintendent, Norman Maycock. Mr Maycock was a strict boss and used to appear on site in his black A30 car, UBM 148, and hide at strategic places to see what was going on. He had two secretaries, Chris Goff and Becky Abrahams.

The most difficult coaches to organise were those for the factory fortnight Saturdays. Dennis and Norman would work until 10.00pm on the Friday to make sure all the arrangements were in place, and would produce large charts or graphs with all the services and numbers of coaches on them. They all used to get into the limited coach bays when they were needed. Dennis and Norman would be at the Bus Station at 5.00am to check each vehicle in, and Dennis had to label each duplicate coach to its destination. All the local coach operators used to help out, and their vehicles would also have a label stating that 'This vehicle is on hire to United Counties'.

Passengers started to arrive at 7.00am and all coaches had left by 9.00am. The service buses had to work round these arrangements; as soon as they arrived they were either put straight into a bay or out of the way on the outside parking area.

After 9.00am Dennis used to go home for a rest, and would sometimes be expected to return for the early morning shift on Sunday as well. He was sometimes asked to work on Boxing Day, where he was supposed to supervise the inspectors, including Sam and Wally Cockerill. These men were much more able to organise themselves and he wondered if they resented him being there to boss them about.

Buses on the Duston routes 321/322 were mainly the reserve of older vehicles. The route was only 4.6 miles long; if an older bus broke down it was thus quicker to send out a replacement and the engineers did not have far to go to tow in the breakdown.

One of the conductors at Derngate, Bill Meredith, was a keen photographer, and his photographs are sought after for publications far and wide for their historic accuracy and clarity.

In 1961 Dennis decided to move and got a job at British Timken, in the export sales department, Asia branch. He worked there for 25 years before taking early retirement. He then worked for a nut and bolt company on Brackmills Industrial Estate before being made redundant.

Dennis has always been a bus enthusiast and keeps a keen eye on the local bus scene. He enjoys using his bus pass to go into town when he wants, and has helped out fellow enthusiast Graham Ledger with his restorations of Bristols 838 and 869, including keeping the ingrained cement dust off one of them.

One unusual incident was when the new Bristol VR buses started to come into the fleet. These had a new gear-changing system and not all drivers could cope with them. One day 757, allocated at that time to Northampton, was resting by the back of the Café with its front facing the bus bays on the other side of the bus station. Its next driver accidentally selected reverse gear and wondered why the bus did not move when he let the brake off. The engine at the back was vibrating the wall of the Café instead of pushing the bus forward. The driver was suspended and the rest of the staff came out on strike. Norman Maycock had to sort it out. The bus retired to Eastern Coach Works, at Lowestoft, for substantial repair and was moved to Wellingborough, then on to Biggleswade before being preserved by John Robertson.

Dennis is looking forward to the new MAN buses arriving for Stagecoach, and hopes that they will be useful vehicles.

Steve Loveridge

I started work at the United Counties Bedford Road Head Office on 6 January 1969, when United Counties had just become part of the National Bus Company. My first job was as a clerk in the Licensing Department of the Traffic Office, where I spent most of my time checking the weekly 'Notices and Proceedings', in which all applications for service changes of all local operators appeared. There were four of these to check, for the Eastern, East Midland, Metropolitan and South Eastern Traffic Areas. Any service or excursion variation concerning any operator in the United Counties area was noted and entered in the huge ledgers, with all the relevant details. I also assisted with the applications to the Traffic Commissioners to change timetables and fare tables when we had a fare increase.

There were 13 staff in the Traffic Office at the time, and more than 100 at Head Office altogether, compared with the current Head Office staff of fewer than 20. There was a Chief Traffic Assistant, Tom White, and Publicity Officer Bob Whiteley. Bob had three Traffic Assistants, John Harris, Nellie Marlow and Phyllis Brittain. Also in the office were Bob Coote, the Licensing and Fares Officer, Frank Bell and myself. Mrs Allen worked on the School Term tickets with Nora Brown. Percy Grieves was the Schedules and Development Officer and Ian Gentles assisted the Traffic Manager with work on special projects. Geoff Mantle was the Machine Room Operator, who copied all the duties and car graphs and Roneo'd

the staff notices and other stencils, as there were no photocopiers in those days. Joe Beckett, the Driving Examiner, and Lew Chapman, the Chief Inspector, also had desks in the office.

In 1971 I was asked to go to Bedford, in the Schedules Office, with Dave 'Bomber' Harris, from whom I learned a great deal and to whom I will always be thankful for teaching me all I know about scheduling.

Maurice Jewitt was the District Traffic Superintendent at Bedford, and as a young man I had great respect for him. If you were wrong you were told so and you accepted the decision that he had made. If you were right he would back you to the hilt. Les Bidewell was the Chief Clerk and always wore leather-soled shoes; he would rush along the corridor, grab the doorframe of the office he wanted and slide in!

At Bedford, when I was 18 I passed as a conductor and got the badge. I was soon out on the road in the evenings and at weekends. At this time we were desperately short of staff and I worked at virtually all of the United Counties depots – my favourites were Huntingdon, Rushden and Wellingborough. There was many a day when I did a morning peak bus from Rushden to Bedford, worked all day on Bedford town services, then finished off at Wellingborough on the 'Last Wash House' (the 11.05pm from Wellingborough to the Irthlingborough Co-op Laundry). There were eight shifts and a late spare at the time at Wellingborough, and we ran to Kettering, Irthlingborough, Northampton, Raunds, Doddington, Bozeat and both Queensway and Berrymoor Estates. Most of these runs were crew-operated with Bristol Lodekkas of the LD, FS or FLF variants, or one-person-operated (OPOs) with Bristol REs. We also had one of the former Birch Bros Leyland Leopards, DUC 70C, which went like a rocket and usually worked the last Raunds run. When Leyland Nationals were delivered in 1973, they were used on most of the late turns, but some of the old-hand drivers preferred the double-deckers, as I did, and I would use one if they wanted. Little did I realise then that 35 years later I would regularly conduct on Bristol FLFs on stage services.

It was while travelling to and from Bedford, every day, that I first set eyes on the love of my life. No, not my future wife but Bristol VRT 794 (GRP 794L), which regularly operated one of the first one-man duties from Kettering, a Desborough outstation duty, the 8.00am from Rushden to Kettering. Thirty-odd years later I would be instrumental in helping to preserve it.

I transferred back to Bedford Road in 1973, and after a while I was appointed as Licensing and Fares Officer, a position I held until I moved to Kettering to take up the job of Schedules and Development Officer in 1978. I stayed there for more than 20 years, compiling schedules for Wellingborough, Kettering,

Bristol VRT 794 in Kettering Town Centre for a Road Safety campaign in 1992. *David March collection*

Corby and Stamford depots and outstations, although both Wellingborough and Stamford would eventually close. This again brought me into contact with 794. When we reopened Thrapston outstation, 794 went there with 811 and became the regular bus of my good friend Roger Smith.

During my time at Kettering I also took responsibility for both Bedford and Huntingdon schedules, due to Dave Harris being off ill for a considerable time.

In 1991 I married Denise, who used to be the telephonist at Bedford when I worked there, and of course the 'wedding car' was 794!

When Bill Smith came back to United Counties as Traffic Manager, after being in Africa and Grimsby (not a lot of difference there, then…), it was decided to recentralise the Schedules Department and form a Commercial Department, with Roger Warwick, Graeme Carr, Howard Butler, Ray Ramsey and myself. We would do all the schedules, timetables, fares and marketing, so for me it was yet another return to Head Office, but this time at Rothersthorpe Avenue.

In 2000 United Counties was merged with Cambus and Viscount to form Stagecoach East, and I had to get to know the Cambridge and Peterborough routes as well as town services in places far away, such as Haverhill and Newmarket. These were very interesting times and getting to know these places and several new faces was a challenge. One of the people I then renewed acquaintance with was Phillip Norwell,

who I knew previously as a driver at Oundle outstation and was now my new boss. We hopefully worked well together and many a scheme was hatched in March, Haverhill or Ely garages, while reprogramming destination blinds, which was usually at some unearthly hour! While we were one company, I was closely involved in helping set up and design the extremely successful Cambridge Citi network.

When the company was reformed and we became Stagecoach East, in just Northamptonshire and Bedfordshire again, we had the choice of keeping one of the two Bristol FLFs, inherited from Cambus/ Viscount, and we kept 19953, the closed-top one. This is now my favourite bus, but I am still allowed to play with 19952 now and again. When I am out with either of these it takes me back to my younger days, in the 1970s, which I believe were the 'glory days' of United Counties (with apologies to Kevin Lane).

By the time you read this I will hopefully have completed my 40 years of service with 'The Company', and have been fortunate to meet many people. There are too many to mention, but one or two deserve to be, and I apologise to those I have missed. They are not in any particular order, but here goes: Stan Morris, for setting me on; John Tate, for taking a chance on giving me the job of Licensing and Fares Officer; Alex Carter; Tom White; Bob Whiteley; Ray Ramsey; Bob Coote; Len Gentle; Maurice Jewitt; Dave Harris; Gerald Mead; Phillip Norwell; Tony Cox; Inglis Lyon; James Freeman; Bill Smith, both father and son; Brian

Hadden; Roger Warwick; Howard
Butler; Graeme Carr; Lyn Worboys;
Michelle Hargreaves; Steve Hamilton;
and finally my wife Denise, who puts up
with my buses both large and small.

I have of course many other
memories, some of which are funny, some
sad, some that can never be told and
some that may be told one day. At the

David Pike and Steve Loveridge
with Bristol FLF open-top 19952
on the 2008 Northampton Balloon
Festival services. *Steve Loveridge
collection*

moment not enough water has passed under Harrold
Bridge to recall these, but you never know, I might put
pen to paper and write a book of my own!

John Appleton

After working at Rushden (see Volume 2), in 1974
John became one of the two Driving Examiners based
at Northampton Head Office, working with Norman
Redhead. Between them they were responsible for the
training and testing of all drivers for United Counties
and were required to attend courses at the MOTEC
Training Centre in Shropshire several times.

When deregulation came to United Counties John
and Norman ceased to be part of the National Bus
Company and were taken over by Stagecoach. They
met Brian Souter and Anne Gloag several times at
Bedford; they were very approachable and would sit

with staff and have lunch in the canteen.

When Norman retired, John became the only
examiner until he retired from this post in 1999.
Originally their office was at the Main Works. They
then moved to Greyfriars Bus Station, from where
they were moved to Milton Keynes for a short time,
being ousted by the new National Express call centre,
returning to Rothersthorpe Avenue.

From his Northampton days, John remembers the
company artist, Bill Goodman, who used to design and
paint all the advertisements used in the company buses
and bus stations. He was instrumental in painting the
buses with the 75-year-anniversary livery.

In later Stagecoach days John trained staff in
Cambridgeshire, Peterborough, Rugby, Leamington
Spa, Coventry and Stratford-upon-Avon. The drivers
from the west would come to Northampton and he
would go to the others.

In his United Counties and Stagecoach days
John worked with Colin Clubb,
John Tate, Barry Warner and Ben
Colson, as well as many other staff
over the years; in the main they all
worked together well with very few
upsets. John had some very good
instructors when he was in charge of
the Driving School, who helped him
tremendously.

John Appleton with Tony
Cassidy in the Driving School
at Northampton. *John Appleton
collection*

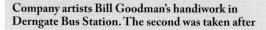

Company artists Bill Goodman's handiwork in Derngate Bus Station. The second was taken after closure, when the bus station was used as a store for surplus grain. *Both Roger Warwick collection*

Graeme Carr

Graeme has been interested in buses since his schooldays. Living near Luton, he went to school not by United Counties or Luton Corporation but by Green Line RF and SMW buses. Moving to Dunstable, he used the 61 Aylesbury to Luton and 71 Leighton Buzzard to Luton routes, with Bristol buses. He remembers that Bristol FLFs were mainly used, but some days anything could be found; in fact, at one time Red & White LS buses were used. Later he remembers a Bristol VR, 780, being used.

In those days the United Counties offices were in Williamson Street, Luton, and were jointly run with Luton Corporation. Graeme started work there in 1975 at the age of 19 as a Junior Management Trainee, taking over from John Broughton, who had just finished his training. United Counties also had graduate trainees, who had come from university.

Graeme was taken on by Brian Horner, who in those days was the Traffic Manager. Starting in November, Graeme was given a pre-Christmas 'baptism of fire', which included two days at Head Office, two days at Northampton, two days at Bedford and two days at Luton, all shadowing the managers at those depots.

Left: **Graeme Carr.** *NBC News*

Above: **The original office block at Luton Depot.** *Roger Warwick collection*

His next training was to be a conductor, then to help out in Schedules at Luton. Graeme was now working in the newer offices at Castle Street, above the MOT bays and next to the canteen. The District Superintendent was Bob Rumbold and Depot Manager was Richard Christian.

In 1977 Graeme moved to spend a year at Bedford. He started at the depot and learned every job there was. He remembers getting to work at 4.00am to check that the depot was up and running and to deal with any shortages of staff or vehicles. The District Superintendent was Maurice Jewitt, and Doug Elphee was the Depot Manager.

Staff shortages were such that office-based staff worked as drivers and conductors on Saturdays. Graeme and Clive Jones used to crew together. In those days Bedford Depot only had a front and side door, and buses came in by the side door and left by the front door. Town buses were parked close together at the back of the depot in two rows, with the country buses parked at the front. All buses were fuelled and washed before being parked up.

His next training was at Northampton Head Office. Graeme spent some time with the engineers in the Works, then in the Ticket Audit Section of Miss Piercy's department of 18 girls and more home-based part-timers. In those days the office staff finished at 5.30pm on Monday to Friday; they all went to get their coats at 5.25 and sat back at their desks until it was time to go. Within this department were based six computer girls; the computer had its own room and was very 'macro' rather than 'micro' in size! Eventually the office purchased a personal computer (PC), and each department had a few hours a day to work on it.

One job that Graeme was given was to audit the ticket machines in the store. Setright machines were used at most depots, with Almex A machines being used at Luton and Hitchin. These machines were originally from all over the country, and local ones were registered with UC or E numbers. Others included former Birch Bros and Red & White machines. Graeme bought a spare machine for £1 plus 8% VAT, and learned to drive buses.

Graeme next transferred to Head office as a Commercial Assistant, working with Roger Warwick for

17 years until Roger retired in 1999. The Commercial Department was part of the Traffic Office, and their work involved licensing vehicles, all fare changes, publicity, timetable preparation, National Express complaints, and helping the Chief Schedules Officer. The team included a typist, who worked in the typing pool. Graeme was one of the first staff to be trained on the personal computer. He produced the fares table and camera-ready artwork ready for the printers (Xpres Printers), also in Bedford Road, Northampton. Before using the computer, all items had to be proof-read before printing.

In 1984 the NBC carried out a survey called 'Bus Driver', which was a similar survey to the 'MAP' of the 1970s. The purpose was to see where the customers were using services and producing new services where required.

United Counties Head Office became the accounting centre for the Midland area of the NBC. When Stagecoach took over in 1987 the new Wayfarer ticket machines were brought into use. Graeme became used to using these machines, as he was still helping out at weekends with driving turns. On Sundays Northampton Transport did not operate, and Stagecoach vehicles did the services instead. This meant that Graeme used to wander round Northampton all day.

In 1988 Stagecoach made redundancies and the Commercial Department was reduced to four people. Trevor Jones and Graham Archer made up the team, with Roger Warwick as the Manager.

At about this time Stagecoach bought a former exhibition bus and converted it to a 'Roadshop'. John Robertson had an HGV licence and was brought over to drive it. This started as a full-time job but was later part-time, and stopped altogether later on. In his spare time John became part of the team. When Trevor Jones

Ticket Audit work with Willibrew tickets. This photograph was taken at Kettering but the work at Northampton was similar. *Roger Warwick collection*

and Graham Archer moved on, John joined the team, now only three, doing the fare changes.

When networked PCs and publishing were developed, the team produced their own publicity material and in some cases also attached it to vehicles and arranged special launches. One of these involved the launching of the B6 vehicles. When the Routemaster runs were started in Bedford and Corby the blinds were made at Chiswick especially for Stagecoach, arranged by the Commercial Department.

Graeme retired in 1995 from full-time commercial work and now works for Stagecoach East in the Timetable Planning Department, commuting between Northampton and Rugby. This work takes about one to two days a week. He also works with Steve Loveridge and Howard Butler driving the Stagecoach restored FLF buses on special runs and events.

John Coleman

John was looking for a job working with figures, and this was his main reason for applying to United Counties for a job. He started work there in 1952 at the Bedford Road Headquarters, then at Derngate Bus Station until 1960, when he went to work in the offices of Cleavers Builders Merchants in Wood Street. He then moved to Norfolk in 1970.

John first worked in the Wages Department, and remembers that his boss was Mr Ward. Later he went to work for Norman Maycock above the Booking Office at Derngate. Part of his job was to organise the coaches for the factory fortnight in Northampton. Some 15 to 20 coaches would be going to Great Yarmouth; these were too many to come into the bus station, so were lined up in the road outside

instead. This would have been on the first Saturday of the two-week holiday.

From those days John remembers George Lucas, who was an Inspector, and George Blunt, who was in charge of the canteen. From football days he remembers Ray Needle, whose father was a bus driver.

When the M1 motorway was under construction, coach trips were organised to Collingtree to see the work in progress.

One day John remembers coming back from Fenny Stratford at about 4.00pm to find that the crews were on strike in Derngate. Police had to be called and they ordered the drivers to release the girls from Derngate High School who were locked inside.

John used to play for the football club based at Bedford Road. Several members of the staff there stated that they were interested in the forming of a football club with a view to entering a team in the Northampton Town League. Contact was made with various players who had previously turned out in a friendly match, and it was established that there was support from approximately 17 players. Consequently Fred Merriman, the Company Secretary, was approached as to whether the company would have any objection to the use of its name. Mr Merriman stated that there would be no objection and he would himself offer every assistance.

On 8 May 1954 an application was made in the name of United Counties Houghton Road Football Club, although at that time it did not officially exist, and the Town League Secretary requested the club to attend a meeting of the Committee for acceptance of new teams into the Town League. This was held at

The United Counties team, with Richard Coleman on the left of the back row. Third from the left is Peter Minney, second from the right is Bert Seaman, and on the extreme right John Buckby. In the front row, on the left is Ray Needle, in the middle is Peter York, and on the extreme right Bob Coote. John Coleman remembers that they had been playing in a Tilling Group game that day. *John Coleman collection*

The Fancier's Club, Wood Street, Northampton, on Tuesday 25 May at 7.30pm. Mr D. Curtis and Mr R. Coote attended the meeting to give personal support to the application.

On 27 May Mr Hockaday, the Town League Secretary, phoned Mr Coote and informed him that the team had been accepted into the Town League Division 3B. Acting on this information, a General Meeting was called for Friday 28 May 1954 in the Works Canteen, Bedford Road, at 5.30pm. The minutes of the meeting were as follows:

Meeting commenced at 5.45pm.
Fourteen members of the staff were in attendance and it was agreed to elect Mr White as Chairman for the evening.
No members from the works were in attendance, but this was possibly caused by the short notification and also the fact that they finished work at 5.00pm and went home.
Mr White stated that a General Committee should be formed in order to get to work in obtaining money for the running of the Club.

In 1957 the club had to change its name to Becketts United, due to the lack of ongoing support from United Counties.

Ben Colson

Ben was brought up in the countryside of Suffolk and went to school in Bury St Edmunds, which was 17 miles from home. His first interest in buses started when he used to go on the Eastern Counties buses driven by a driver called Bill. The 3-mile free bus pass was used by Ben and his mates. The local drivers had differing ways of using this pass. When Bill was driving on a Friday afternoon they would leave their

bicycles 3 miles from home because they knew he would throw them off. On a Tuesday they would not be thrown off as a Bury crew would be driving. Another driver was Ken, who would not turf them off. One Bonfire Night the lads used seats as rocket launchers, then tried to set fire to straw-roofed cottages with fireworks. The crew and the local populous were not amused.

Ben looked for weekend work in Bury. He worked at the Greene King Brewery, making soft drinks and drinking tea rather than the local brew. Brewing was very popular in Suffolk as local farmers used to have a barrel of mild and a second of bitter in the harvest fields, as harvesting was such a dry-mouth job, with all the dust. He was only 16 at the time. This was not what he wanted, so he applied to work at the local bus booking office. He got the job in 1967 and worked on a part-time basis until he left university in 1974. The job was good as he had a free travel pass instead of using the bike.

Ben studied the bus business at London University from 1970. When he graduated he applied to be a management trainee at the National Bus Company, and his training position was at East Midlands Motor Services at Chesterfield. This area, with its coal tips, coke works and smoggy local cities of Sheffield and Rotherham, was quite a culture shock for a country lad from Suffolk.

After two years, in 1976 Ben was appointed nearer home as Assistant District Traffic Superintendent with Eastern Counties at Norwich. With all its outstations and its antiquated management technique, this was a completely different company compared to East Midlands. Two years later, in 1978, Ben moved to Cambridge, as Depot Superintendent. This was to be a turning point in his career as he was forced to revolutionise the local bus system, due to a severe shortage of staff.

After sorting out the local services, Ben and his team redesigned the coaching routes. Coaches were lying spare and commuters wanted a fast and comfortable trip to London. The railways had not improved for years, so there was not much competition. The opening of the M11 motorway also helped, as it cut a journey time from 2hr 45min to 1hr 45min. The service ran frequently during the day at £3.00 return, and became very popular. This is relevant to United Counties as he also introduced a similar idea there, called Coachlinks.

Ben Colson at Rothersthorpe Avenue, Northampton.
Northampton Chronicle and Echo

In 1981 Ben returned to Chesterfield as Assistant Traffic Manager. This job involved much union negotiation and he had to deal with the Passenger Transport Executives of the local councils in Sheffield, Rotherham and Doncaster. Rotherham built a new bus depot and the canteen team walked out, as the company would not pay moving allowances – the new depot was across the road from the old one. The dispute stopped all bus services in those areas for 12 days. Even the PTE boss joined the protest, and East Midlands services were curtailed at the borders of the areas. Ben found it appalling that his customers were deprived of a service for this length of time. As a result he gained experience that he used when dealing with councils and unions at United Counties.

Ben then became Traffic Manager at Southern National at Taunton within 36 hours of applying for the post. Southern National was being created by a split from Western National, and staff morale was poor, due to uncertainty about their future. The experiences gained in this post were very beneficial to Ben when he had to deal with all the uncertainty at United Counties a few years later. One thing Ben remembers from these days was that the whole team got behind him and they achieved much in his three years there. His first car had doors that had to be strung together to keep them shut. Later he had one with normal doors.

One day Ben walked into a door with a filing cabinet behind it, and suffered concussion. He was called to Oxford the next day and interviewed for the Traffic Manager post at United Counties. Much to his surprise he was appointed – surprising as he was concussed at the time, should have been in hospital and was given the wrong set of company figures to evaluate at the interview.

John Tate and John Bodger, the Regional Manager, appointed him. This was a good grounding post and Ben learned such a lot in his five years with United Counties, enabling him to go on and achieve many things later on.

United Counties and Ben went through a vast amount of change and upheaval in those five years. HM Government decided to split up the bus industry by privatising all its parts. This would provide competition, which should have been better for the passengers. United Counties would be split off from Milton Keynes, later becoming Milton Keynes City buses, and the Luton area, later becoming Luton & District buses.

Ben found it strange that he and his thousands of colleagues did not know if they would be in work, or for whom they would be working. Competition with other companies was a new concept and required Ben to throw away conventional thinking and try something new.

At that time the county councils had to cut their transport budgets, one by 25% and the other by 33%. Ben used his former experience with Cambridge Council to negotiate the best deal he could to provide a reasonable standard of service to the Council. He found he could deal with the Councillors better, as he could understand how they ticked. In negotiating a good deal he worked closely with the team from First Bus (the former Northampton Corporation Transport). This built up good working relationships, which were very useful in later challenges he faced. The Government decided that all restructuring of Council-run services should be implemented by October 1986 and they called it D Day. Due to other events taking place locally, Ben and his team implemented theirs in April 1986, which enabled most things to have bedded down by the D Day. So D Day in Northamptonshire and Bedfordshire was a damp squib and Ben decided to go on Concorde to Prague instead.

Also, a management buy-out team had to be established. This included Ben, John Tate and three others. They found this strange, as they had to show all the competitors for the company all their information to make the bidding fair for all. Also, he was not supposed to be helping colleagues bidding for other parts of the company, as they were potential competitors. However, for day-to-day company working he had to forget that and carry on as normally as he could.

United Counties was not doing very well financially at the time and as a result it was decided that the whole network needed restructuring. This involved taking the profitable routes and, by surveying the passenger use, rebuilding them to serve more people who wanted to use them. On the 128 service, the times were improved by providing underused coaches and diverting the route away from underused villages. This enabled the two vehicles used to be more efficient and gave a time reduction, which attracted more commuters. Peterborough to Corby, Kettering, Northampton, Daventry and Birmingham became a very profitable corridor Coachlinks service.

Another profitable route was the Northampton to Wellingborough corridor, with add-on services to Raunds, Higham, Rushden and Irthlingborough. Also included as profitable was the Kettering to Bedford via Rushden corridor and the Northampton to Towcester corridor. All these benefited from quicker Coachlinks services.

Local town services were not profitable in Wellingborough, Kettering and Corby until United Counties introduced the 'Street Shuttle' minibuses, which made the services more flexible and cheapened the overheads. This left the remaining bus services, which were restructured, and the remaining Council-sponsored services. These were all operated by conventional single- and double-deck OMO buses.

The unions were having a very uneasy period, where they were challenging many of the decisions Ben made. Feelings ran high and Ben was at the end of some very rude and hurtful rhetoric from the union side. This affected him very much and as a result he learned to deal with his colleagues better without the use of union backing.

Ben attended the announcement of the successful bidder for the company. The management buy-out team were told that they had not been successful, and they met again their new boss Brian Souter. Brian made a very good impression on Ben and they worked together full-time for the next 10 years, and at the time of writing occasionally still do. Brian said, 'I am the new boss now. I am impressed with what you all have done over the last few months. You need a break – go away and come back to run the company refreshed.'

However, when Stagecoach took over in 1987 Brian decided that he could not run an efficient bus service with all the restrictive practices still in place. The management team negotiated with the unions and eventually this was resolved. Ben remembers particularly his negotiating with union men Stock and Garner. This conclusion enabled the management team to update the company, as they needed to do, to ensure its survival in a competitive market. Brian's vision was to increase the number of people using the buses so that they would become profitable. This was unheard of in NBC days. Brian Souter was a 'people person'.

Ben left Stagecoach United Counties in 1989 to take up a post at the much bigger Ribble, which was also in the Stagecoach group by then. After that he was a member of the special project team at Stagecoach working in Hong Kong, New Zealand and the USA.

He returned in 1995 and bought a small company in Norfolk called Norfolk Green. At the time of writing it runs 55 buses in an area from near Peterborough to Cromer and south to Norwich. The company has no union, but any employee can talk to Ben and sort out his or her problems.

Ben negotiates with Norfolk County Council, which enables him to provide the services it needs profitably. One of these profitable routes is along the North Norfolk coast, where at peak times extra vehicles are needed.

Ben is a management trainer for Stagecoach, and is also a representative for smaller operators on the Government lobby for the bus industry. He spends time negotiating with politicians and feels more comfortable now than when he was doing so in East Midland days.

Ben has also written a book on the history of the Royal Station at Wolferton, near the Queen's Sandringham home. This book is sold to fund the local Scarecrow celebrations in the village.

The main Works entrance in United Counties Engineering days. *Roger Warwick collection*

2
Bedford Road Central Works
(United Counties Engineering)

L ocated next door to Head Office, this facility was expanded over the years and eventually became United Counties Engineering, being sold separately with other National Bus Company engineering works.

At the front of the building, facing Bedford Road, was the depot building for Northampton. Most crews were based at Derngate Bus Station and the depot building was mainly used for overflow vehicles and coaches. However, some official staff cars were also housed in the building. There was also a small canteen.

Staff at the Central Works were able to build and refurbish most vehicles, including their own breakdown tenders and a couple of rafts for charity races on the River Nene, which flowed close by. Staff at the Works had their own social scene, with football, skittles and darts leagues, while charity events included pushing a single-decker bus round nearby Billing Aquadrome.

The Central Works main pits, with fitters working on the right. *Roger Warwick collection*

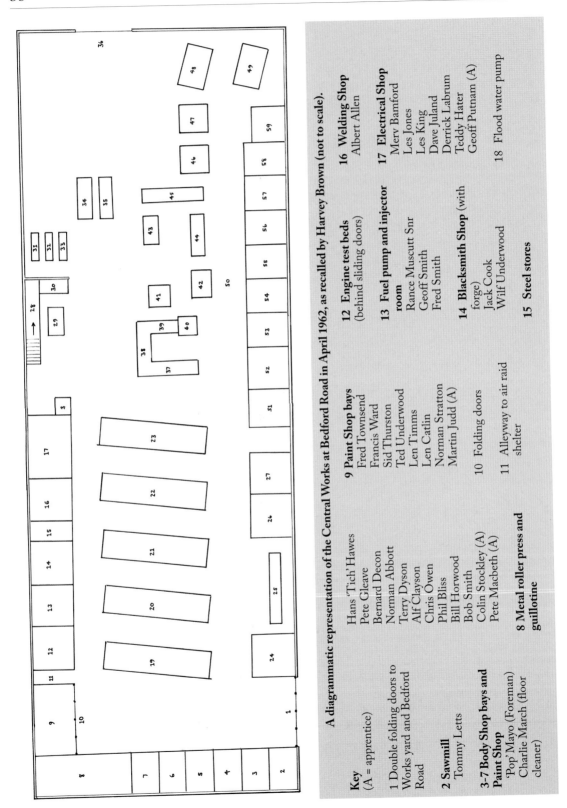

A diagrammatic representation of the Central Works at Bedford Road in April 1962, as recalled by Harvey Brown (not to scale).

Key
(A = apprentice)

1 Double folding doors to Works yard and Bedford Road

2 Sawmill
Tommy Letts

3-7 Body Shop bays and Paint Shop
'Pop' Mayo (Foreman)
Charlie March (floor cleaner)

Hans 'Tich' Hawes
Pete Gleave
Bernard Decon
Norman Abbott
Terry Dyson
Alf Clayson
Chris Owen
Phil Bliss
Bill Horwood
Bob Smith
Colin Stockley (A)
Pete Macbeth (A)

8 Metal roller press and guillotine

9 Paint Shop bays
Fred Townsend
Francis Ward
Sid Thurston
Ted Underwood
Len Timms
Len Catlin
Norman Stratton
Martin Judd (A)

10 Folding doors

11 Alleyway to air raid shelter

12 Engine test beds (behind sliding doors)

13 Fuel pump and injector room
Rance Muscutt Snr
Geoff Smith
Fred Smith

14 Blacksmith Shop (with forge)
Jack Cook
Wilf Underwood

15 Steel stores

16 Welding Shop
Albert Allen

17 Electrical Shop
Merv Bamford
Les Jones
Les King
Dave Juland
Derrick Labrum
Teddy Hater
Geoff Putnam (A)

18 Flood water pump

19-23 Dock Shop area
Harold Allchin (Foreman)
George Smith (floor cleaner)
Bert Brown (floor cleaner)

19 Pit No 1: service pit
Frank Davis (fitter)
Johnny Legge (A)
Bill Darby (front axle dock)
'Father' McGinty (back axle dock)

Harry Jelly (floating fitter)

20 Pit No 2: service pit
Dave Miles (fitter)
Tom Cripps (A)
Bill Benson and
Ron Labrum (back axle dock)

21 Pit No 3: crash repair pit

22 Pit No 4: premature failure pit

23 Pit No 5: overhaul pit
Norman Reeves and others

24 Works Office
Sid Wesley (Works Superintendent)
Ernie Hughes (clerk)

25 Tyre and wheel rack

26 Body Shop stores
27 Engineer stores
George Marriott
Johnny Walsh
Tom York

28 Stairs up to toilets, washroom and canteen, and along landing to Trim Shop
Alf Bland
Bert Morgan
Dickie Dunkeley
Colin Gardner
John Cunningham
Les Trazler
Mick ?
Les Porter (A)
Martin Worrall (A)
'Smithy' (A)

29 Staff car service pit
Bill Law

30 Fitter's bench

31-33 Degreasing and cleaning area
Mr Scott 'Old Ben'
31 Paraffin
32 Wash tank
33 Turco (very strong chemical cleaner requiring the use of heavy rubber gloves)

34 Engine stripping bay

35 Axle stripping bay

36 Doors to Northampton Depot

37-41 Overhaul section

37 Front axle overhaul
Ernie Ginger
'Shag' Stephens

38 Cylinder head overhaul
Bert Smith

39 Water pumps, exhauster pumps (air brakes) and steering boxes overhaul
Joe Hall

40 Water tank

41 Main servo overhaul

42-49 Machine Shop
Wilf Johnstone (Foreman)

42 Brake drum grinder

43 Cylinder block press
44 Crankshaft grinder
45 Cylinder borer
Ken Cross

46 General use grinder

47 Vertical miller and grinder

48 Lathe 1
Herbert Oxley

49 Lathe 2
Dennis Allen
Terry Green (A)

50 Walkway

51 Gearbox bench
Ollie Collins
Gordon Heard
Ian Inwood
Spike Tulinski (A)

52 Back axle bench
Dave Hollowell
Tom Hopkins
Harry Harrison
Albert Green

53 No 1 engine bench
Brian Savage

54 No 2 engine bench
Johnny Gibson
Pete Griffiths (A)

55 No 3 engine bench
Keith Snedker
Harvey Brown (A)

56 No 4 engine bench
Stuart Woodford
Allen Dunkley

57 Con-rod preparation
Sam Thompson

58 Crankcase preparation
Jimmy Edwards
Brian Ward

59 First Aid post

Colin Clubb takes Luton officials round the Central Works in 1976. Ian Wilson is working on a gearbox while Jock Mitchell, in the middle, explains the workings. *Colin Clubb collection*

Engineers Ian Wilkins, Bob Slade, Andrew Huggett, Robbie McKenzie, Rob Prested and Alan Bates in United Counties Engineering days, when their skills were also used by other companies and charities. *Northampton Chronicle and Echo*

Geoff Pullin

Geoff originates from Clevedon near Bristol. He left Liverpool University in 1962 and joined Bristol Commercial Vehicles in Chatsworth Road, Brislington, as an apprentice. This involved working in the drawing office, including the designing of the back axle suspension on the Bristol RE single-deckers.

Geoff became a graduate trainee with the Tilling group and worked at the Bristol Omnibus Company, which involved section and traffic training.

In 1965 Geoff moved to Eastern Counties at Norwich as Assistant to the Engineer. At this time the company was a low-cost operation and his duties included going round to the 45 outstations changing light bulbs, oiling doors, cleaning signs and any other small jobs. Promotion came in 1967 to Area Engineer at Norwich and Ipswich. Geoff worked at the Central Works, where he helped to set up a cyclical maintenance scheme. He also moved the apprentices about to give them more experience of different areas of work.

His next job was at Maidstone & District, which, being a BET company, had much more money. Arthur White was the General Manager and he used to buy 50-plus buses at a time compared to a few at a time for Tilling companies. Geoff used tact and diplomacy to implement a work study into the stores function. This job gave Geoff a good insight into tyres and the various makes (Michelin, Dunlop and Firestone).

From 1972 to 1978 Geoff was with Ribble as Assistant Chief Engineer under Harry Turner. Bristol REs were the largest order, then Leyland Nationals arrived with 680 engines. One National was also tested with electric power.

In 1978 Geoff went to United Counties, with Colin Clubb as General Manager. His company car was a Triumph Herald 2.5. One of his first jobs was to rationalise the company depots; as a result Rushden, Desborough and Stamford depots closed. On his visit to Desborough he found that

the depot was being run by the cleaner that day, who seemed glad that he was going to be made redundant. Geoff arranged an update at Wellingborough Depot and upgraded facilities at Bedford and Luton. Bletchley Depot was now in the adapted bakery (see Volume 2).

Geoff worked with John Tate and his new team to design and build the new depot at Winterhill, Milton Keynes. The brief was to produce an upside-down biscuit-tin-shaped building, which would look pretty and service 150 buses. The depot had to include 15 pits, a running shift, access to both sides of the building and a PSV testing station. In fact, the building was very underused, painters being bussed down from Northampton to use up space. The main vehicles to use the depot were Bristol VRs. Peter Adams was appointed as Assistant Chief Engineer. He later started his own company fitting air-conditioning to coaches, having done this with United Counties.

Geoff's next job was to sort out the mess at Luton, where Geoff found that 40 vehicles were out of traffic at any one time. The maintenance regime was updated and a new Area Engineer, from the Post Office, appointed who turned the depot around. The Luton site was very restricted and there was no spares storage and supply system. Sunday maintenance was also introduced, and Luton became a centre of excellence under Jim Weeks and John Whiton. Ten months was spent in changing engines to make the vehicles more reliable. At this time a full motorway recovery service was established.

Back at Northampton, Jim Foreman was building Leyland engines to replace Bristol engines. Ted Vickery was the Engineering Officer and every vehicle had its own maintenance record introduced.

Geoff also upgraded the apprentice regime. All depots had apprentices and they spent some time at

Norman Fowler MP (fifth from the left) visited the Works on 2 May 1980. Also present (l-r) are Geoff Pullin, Peter Brundle, Robert Brook, Irwin Dalton, John Tate, Lord Shepherd and Frank Phillips. *Geoff Pullin collection*

the Central Works and technical college. The Industry Training Board was very unpopular and the regular staff went on strike, as they did not want to waste time training new staff. Jim Foreman became the manager in charge, and vehicles were supplied by the company. Later this work moved to Tile Hill College at Coventry. Dennis Ord also helped with this work.

In the early 1980s Nicholas Ridley privatised the British Road Services nationalised freight industry, and the word was that the bus industry was next. John Tate and the board split the engineering side from the operational side of the business, and it eventually became United Counties Engineering Limited, with Geoff as Manager. The main work came from United Counties, but other companies were serviced, such as the Post Office and other Tilling companies. The company was very efficient and had a good parts supply network; it also started the air-conditioning of vehicles.

On the operational side, the company was divided into two and fleet engineers were appointed. Later

it became three companies. The engineering side was sold to Robert Beattie, who in turn sold it to VanCrown Engineering. It was subsequently run down and closed in 1990, leaving Geoff without a job.

After a year with Derby buses Geoff moved to Tile Hill College as head of PSV training and has now retired.

Other colleagues were Stan Simons, work-study officer, and Freddy Dark, Director of United Counties Omnibus Ltd and later Regional executive of the NBC.

Bill Horwood

Bill ran the Body Shop at Bedford Road Works for United Counties in his later years, but had started work in 1952 as an apprentice, rising to chargehand then Superintendent, from which post he retired from Bedford Road.

He remembers that the Chief Engineer was Geoff Pullin, and that his apprenticeship lasted six years and initially he was paid £1 10s a week. He had to go to technical college on day release for one day and three nights a week.

As Superintendent he managed four departments (Paint Shop, Body Shop, Trim Shop and Fibreglass Shop) and in 1986 had 81 staff.

Bill's favourite coach body was the Plaxton, and he went to Scarborough many times. An old bus was used to store his Plaxton spares, hidden from other managers. He also remembers that the main timbers used in Eastern Coach Works bodies were ash and oak, but they also used a wood called carrowin.

Above: **Bill Horwood (left) and Norman Abbott.** *Denise Abbott collection*

Right: **Bill (centre front with striped jumper) is relaxing with colleagues. Others that can be identified are Peter Gleave (in front of cupboard) and Alf Clayson on the extreme right. The lad on the left seems to be a learner, maybe going out on a driving lesson.** *Denise Abbott collection*

Bill cannot remember individual vehicles in the fleet, as he knew them by their body and chassis numbers and, as there were 500-plus vehicles, he only dealt with the ones needing treatment at any one time.

Jim Foreman

I was born in Stamford, where most of the family were engineers, working at Blackstones Engineering in the town. Harold Blackstone sold the company to J. P. Lister, two clauses in the agreement stating that all the apprentices should be trained the 'Blackstone way' and that the Blackstone name should appear in a set position on the company's petrol engines.

Ten boys and two girls made up the apprentices, supervised by Jimmy Evans, and the apprenticeship lasted five years. If you stepped out of line you would clean the precision equipment in the viewing bay, and were trained by the inspection team to use it as you cleaned it. This team was a good source of engineering drawings; I was interested in these and did a course at night school to produce them.

I had a lot of arguments with my father, who always thought that I should be perfect. I had reached Tool Room training when I decided to join the RAF, so I went to Lincoln for my medical and answered a load of questions. My father tried to stop me from going, but the company listened and allowed me to go subject to honouring a clause in my agreement.

Some years later, after war service and a period with the Bristol Aircraft Company at Filton, I received a letter from a former Corporal I had met in the RAF, inviting me to Northampton for the weekend. By chance I saw an advertisement in the *Chronicle and Echo* that Saturday, saying that Reg Mitchell at United Counties wanted staff. I arrived at the Works through the depot end and was not impressed. However, I asked for Reg and met Gordon Heard, who took me to Reg's office. Chief Engineer George Sell was also there. They looked at my credentials, Reg asked me some technical questions, then offered me a job starting two weeks later. They asked me if I was passing through, as they did not want me to start then go off to another job shortly afterwards. Having reassured them I was not passing through I started a new career.

My first job was the engine in a Bristol LS bus. My neighbour was Frank Davis, who was working on the engine from a Bristol RE at the time. I adjusted to the job well and liked it. I found that the apprentices seemed to be of varying standards. The AUEW was looking for another shop steward and I applied and was voted in.

The apprentices should have been working to a Road Transport Industry Training Board (RTITB) regime. However, it appeared that they were not carrying out the task paperwork required by this scheme, and some had lost their training books. I discussed the situation with John Gibson and Brian Ward, suggesting that we ought to question the way training was taking place. We had a joint meeting with the TGWU and all went to see Reg Mitchell and Gordon Heard.

We were unable to reach an agreement. However, we did agree to inform the Chief Engineer. I was elected to meet with him and show him the evidence I had collected, and he raised no objection to the RTITB coming in to help sort out the problems. It appeared that the scheme was variable in different companies, but I thought it very outdated and reported as such back to my union colleagues. Norman Abbott from the TGWU and I were elected to sort out the mess. I was elected Chairperson of the shop stewards committee.

At this time the Chief Engineer changed and Geoff Pullin arrived to take up the post. Geoff adopted a different system of communication, which meant that we could work together. The unions met monthly with Geoff; I was given the union information while Geoff gathered the management information and we then discussed the items together.

Geoff was in favour of training and he agreed with most of the points we raised. However, two points were not agreed. I suggested that a Head of Training be appointed to control the task. This person should be qualified to set an industry standard and work to achieve it, and the work should include college training where a set standard and positive assessment were carried out.

The system was tested when I was given three new apprentices on my Engine Overhaul section. As a result I was isolated from the rest of my shop stewards. Two of them from the AUEW were not happy, and requested the union members to walk out. Norman Abbott and I left the works together, and the apprentices were left to run the factory, but I checked that they were all right before we went.

I had a talk with Reg Mitchell, then talked to the members who had started picketing the works. Both unions called in their local full-time officials who stated that they were not surprised when their members came out. The stoppage lasted a week, during which I kept hinting that we needed a training room designated for the task, but this hint fell on deaf ears.

After the week the management agreed to a training regime, but no one was appointed to look after it. Just after that the bus industry was privatised by Margaret Thatcher, who saw no reason for the RTITB and abolished it. I went on holiday and when I returned I met with Geoff Pullin. On the way I was accosted by three of the apprentices, stating that they hoped I did not get the job as their lives would not be so easy if I did.

Unfortunately for them I was appointed as Craft Training Officer, using the basics of the training system I had gone through in the RAF.

Each apprentice was assessed by an independent body near the end of his apprenticeship. A major change was that the apprentices in works and depots had the same regime, whereas before depots were different. The Bus & Coach Council (BABC) became the governing body for training, and the whole training plan was written by Tile Hill College in Coventry. Geoff Pullin passed on information to make sure that United Counties was working in line with this plan. I attended the BABC meetings, which

United Counties apprentice John Cunningham (second from right) with other local company apprentices and lecturers at a competition. *Jim Foreman collection*

I found gave me a wider picture of the bus industry. The plan took many years to achieve and we worked closely with Wellingborough Technical College, with apprentices going on a day release basis. I worked closely with John Brown, the college's Head of Faculty, who I found was good at his job and very helpful.

At the Works we had an excellent gearbox section run by Jeff Stainwright and Tony Blunt. I suggested to Geoff Pullin that all auto electricians should receive training on the hydrocyclic gearboxes as they had an electronic control box, which was complicated to understand, to cut out faulty diagnosis. John Brown was able to arrange a week's training, which Geoff agreed.

At Wellingborough College some of the apprentices, two of which were mine, were not tidying up their mess after classes. I went over and gave them a lecture on workshop cleanliness and they all got the picture that it was in their own interests to abide by the rules.

When the Leyland National bus was introduced I organised type training for all relevant skilled staff at the Leyland factory in Lancashire. Geoff Smith and I attended the course on fuel injection, where I raised the old subject of air-to-fuel ratio, which was a throwback to my Filton days.

As the depots were involved in the apprentice training scheme, I had a wider view of the way the system was working. At one stage the company had 38 apprentices. I changed the entry system to enable all apprentices to take the same entry test, which was taken at the college and was used by many leading companies. The results arrived on my desk with a rating A to E. Any with A or B results were likely

candidates, C was a person with potential who could be given a chance, and D and E were not taken on. I helped to carry out interviews in the role of checking school reports, making notes and providing advice.

The depot apprentices spent two years at the depot, then a year at the Works before going back. The Works apprentices did their third year at the depots. If depots were short of staff, third- and fourth-year apprentices were sent out to help.

In later years Peter Grimes arrived at Wellingborough as Area Engineer North and we discussed training quite a bit. Unfortunately, shortly afterwards we lost one of the most promising apprentices at Wellingborough, Martin Brown. Martin had completed his training and I had arranged his assessment. He asked me for extra training, which I allowed him to do prior to his assessment. On the last day he came to see me, had a chat, and went on his way home. I was convinced that we had trained a first-rate engineer. That was the last time I saw him, as he died in a road accident on his way home. Martin was a quiet person but well-liked at Wellingborough. He was also popular in the Hell's Angels set, as Peter Grimes and I found out at his funeral. Bikers attended from all parts of the country and requested to carry his coffin to the church, a request to which his family agreed. The way they did it reminded me of a military funeral in its precision, and they carried him to his final resting place in the same manner. Martin's parents requested that a memorial be set up to his memory and I organised the Martin Brown Trophy for the top apprentice each year. I in turn produced a more challenging system to enable an apprentice to obtain the trophy. The system entailed an assessment of all exams and practical work to a high standard, with supervisory data recording from skilled workers and supervisors. The final part was my assessment at the end of training.

Many of the apprentices were outstanding and took part in competitions entered by the college. This gave the college and the company a good reputation for excellent training. Works apprentices at the top level were Neil Wilmin, John and Stuart Cunningham and Ian Rhodes. From the depots Stephen Riddle from Wellingborough was also in this elite group.

The Body Shop apprentices showed their worth when a new Bristol VR went under a low bridge on the Northampton Road in Kettering and lost its roof. It was on delivery and had not even had a passenger on it. Norman Abbott and new apprentice Clive Faulkner removed the damaged body and replaced it with a new one sent from Lowestoft. This became a major task and they had help from all other trades at the Works to achieve it.

Another apprentice project was a 1913 Charabus, owned by Mike Sutcliffe at Dunstable. Mike had scoured the county for old bodies and engines to reconstruct the vehicle, and it was in an advanced stage of rebuilding when we got it. It arrived with a rough manual and three engines from which to make one good one. Neil Wilmin was project leader. His first job was to blast clean all three engines and select the best one. This machine then received a full rebuild, with the crankcase going to a specialist company for renovation. I explained that the crank had to be hand-fitted into the white metal bearing, demonstrating the hand scraper

technique I had learned at Blackstones, and the use of marking blue. The project took some time but in the end I was satisfied that all was in order. I also had to talk to a specialist company about the piston rings. The magneto was a headache at it had a hand-controlled retard fitted to the steering column. On testing the one problem was that the thing would not start. However, Jeff Stainwright came up with a tool that coupled up to the engine and gave it more inertia to turn over. The engine started and worked well, starting on the handle every time. It was eventually fitted into place and the vehicle completed the London to Brighton rally without faults, at an admitted sedate pace of 7 miles an hour.

At weekends I joined the Bristol bus preservation group at RAF Chelveston with another of my United Counties colleagues, John Appleton. The Americans had used the base during the war, its claim to fame being that Glenn Miller and his band had played there once. John and his colleagues had gathered quite a fleet of vehicles, including a Bristol J, for which I rebuilt the AVW engine. Tony worked on that with me. They bought three engines from a scrapyard and we had a comfortable building to work in and a runway on

which to test the vehicle.

I was sad at the loss of another friend and colleague on the M1 motorway, who was killed in an accident when a lorry hit the recovery truck, which was parked behind Charlie Briggs and he was caught between that and the bus he was sorting out. He had no chance of survival. I had first met him in a pub, when he was overhauling milk floats for a living, and persuaded him to come and work for United Counties. On the day of the accident three Leyland Leopard coaches were coming down to Northampton and one ran out of fuel. The others carried on to base. Charlie went out on a routine breakdown with poor visibility and never came back. The lorry driver stated that the hazard lights on the breakdown truck were not working. I was sceptical of this but it was agreed by two independent witnesses. After the accident the breakdown vehicle was parked outside my office window and on investigation I found that a well-built person, such as Charlie, could accidentally trip the switch on the steering column that controlled the hazard warning lights. I further concluded that the lorry must have wandered onto the hard shoulder to collide with the truck. Peter Adams was the Assistant Chief Engineer at the time, and asked me to write a breakdown procedure to prevent this happening again. While it had some good points, others were not so good, so I had a day with the motorway police on the M1, learned much and rewrote the policy as a result. I asked Richard Dyball, Northampton Depot Engineer, if he wanted the vehicle to be rebuilt by the apprentices. Richard put it to the vote and it was agreed by his staff.

The vehicle was stripped to its bare chassis and, as

the problems was keeping the vehicle to its required weight limit. Eventually it was completed and returned to Northampton Depot next door.

My job was becoming very busy with projects and competitions, meetings at Tile Hill, meetings of the Bus & Coach Council, and many discussions on assessors and assessing. I found that the latter two points were the backbone of all training, and was eventually pleased with the results. When National Vocational Training raised its head some staff were worried that they would lose their jobs as a result of failing these exams, but their fears were unfounded. I signed off the NVQ procedure the last week I was at Northampton Works before retirement.

Before my retirement Peter Grimes and Richard Dyball had moved to the new Luton & District Bus Company. Peter suggested that I go there with the new procedure and set it up for them. While I was sure it would work we had not had time to test the idea, so this gave me a chance to do that. I had a talk with my family and set off for Luton. Training there had been part of my remit before the break-up of the company, so I had some idea of what I was taking on. I decided to join them after a holiday break and that one of the options was to get the training done to Assessment Centre standards. The main problem was to find the assessors to do the work to the required standard for the Bus & Coach Council.

In the meantime another project appeared. Luton & District had taken over a celebrity bus, a Leyland Titan, which required rebuilding to roadworthy standards. There was a lot to do and it took two years to achieve an acceptable result.

Once the vehicle was complete it went on the Pennine Run; an apprentice and I changed the clutch the night before. The bus was soon winning cups at bus rallies.

One of the key areas of training

you can see from the photographs, all units were overhauled by the apprentices with regard to the auto electrics. I explained to them the principles of aircraft overhead control systems and this method was adopted for the truck. One of

Before and after photographs of the breakdown truck following the accident on the M1. *Both Jim Foreman collection*

was gearbox overhaul and, with quite a few failures noted, Jeff Stainwright was contacted by Peter and Richard and hired to sort them out. Jeff came to Luton and shared the training area with me, but moved on to his own workshop in Dunstable later. Later still Luton & District took over the Watford area of Country Bus and a hydrocyclic gearbox expert was found there; he carried out this

Luton & District apprentices with their restored Leyland Titan, seen outside the Luton workshop. *Jim Foreman collection*

work from then onwards.

In the meantime the assessors had finished their training and had been passed out by the Bus & Coach Council, which enabled the company to become an assessment centre. The only change made was that the parents of each candidate were invited to the works to see what a skilled engineer did and ask questions. Having passed all my exams, I was able to pass on my

The Leyland Titan at a bus rally with its proud driver and a cup it won. *Jim Foreman collection*.

knowledge to help others do the same.

One pleasant memory was when Geoff Pullin invited me up to Tile Hill College, where he had become a lecturer, to see the layout. I approved of his work. I suggested to Richard that Luton use Tile Hill as a training centre and he agreed. I monitored the apprentices' progress and Richard checked all the reports.

It would be difficult for me to remember all the apprentices that I trained; however, I estimate that 126 of them were trained successfully with only five failures who did not attain the high standard required.

One apprentice at Bedford did a two-year course in one year and came to Luton for a while on loan. An auto electrician won the Martin Brown Trophy that year, just beating another who spent a spell as the Technical Assistant for Richard Dyball before joining Bedfordshire Police.

One of the apprentices at Milton Keynes, whose father was a bank manager, joined my old friends in the RAF. The RAF required a report from me, complete with my old rank and staff number. As he was a good apprentice this was not a problem, and he later went on to qualify as a Weapons Technician.

Whatever job you do you will get sly remarks from your colleagues, who do not know your background. The late Tommy Tate was underrated, but as my deputy before and after his retirement he was very good. Tommy and I used to help any apprentice having trouble with their exams to make sure they had the key points covered.

By this time I was well known at Tile Hill College with my work at the Bus & Coach Council. Northampton Body Builders College did not have a good reputation, so I changed the apprentices to a college at Portsmouth Depot being run by Harold Bedford. Harold ran a tight ship and we got on well. I wondered why we did not get many takers for that course, but it was probably because it was a long way away.

My working life has been a long road to travel, and in the end I thought it was time to get off the road and retire again to Northampton.

Jim having a well-earned break. *Jim Foreman collection*

Norman Abbott

The following account has been supplied by Norman's daughter Denise.

Norman Abbott was born in Castle Ashby. His father was an electrician and relief chauffeur to Lord Northampton and his mother was a lady's maid at Grendon Hall before they married.

Norman joined United Counties in 1953 and worked in the Body Shop for the bus company and United Counties Engineering. There were a couple of years when he worked for Horton Coach Works. Eventually the works became a part of VanCrown Engineering, before being closed down in 1990.

His contract of employment was not issued until October 1964, when it stated that his grade was BM SLZ. He would be paid for each week's work on the Friday of the following week, and had to produce a medical certificate after three days' absence; the company would not pay employees if sick or injured. After 26 continuous weeks he was entitled to one week's notice of dismissal; this increased to two weeks after two years' service, and four weeks after five years' service.

Norman worked in the Central Works, next door to the running works for Northampton Depot, ultimately receiving two awards for 25 and 35 years of service. He became a Shop Steward, Senior Shop

Above left: **Norman in his office/restroom at the Central Works.** *Denise Abbott collection*

Above right **Alf Clayson, Norman Abbott, Bernard Deacon and two unknown colleagues in the Body Shop in the 1960s.** *Bus & Coach magazine, Denise Abbott collection*

A celebration of 25 years service in 1981. The back row includes Ray Wakeling, Reg Smith, Les Marsh, Richard Dunkeley, Norman Abbott (fifth from left), Gordon Heard, Jeff Smith, Nick Berry, John Tate, Ron Faulkner and Peter Clack. The front row includes Fred Dark and Cath Farley. *Denise Abbott collection*

Steward, then Branch Secretary of the TGWU 5/924, which consisted of United Counties and Airflow Streamline. Other union officials were Eric Stock, Reg Ward (District Secretary of the AUEW), George Walden (District Secretary), and bus driver, then District Secretary and National Secretary Bill (later Lord) Morris. Mr Morris drove Corporation buses. Jim Foreman was the Treasurer of one of the unions.

At one particularly tense meeting with management, the Chief Engineer became agitated and broke many pencils in half in frustration at the union demands.

Denise remembers the strikes. One she remembers best, and was photographed, was when the strikers were enjoying the weather sitting in deckchairs in the park opposite the Central Works side entrance. Norman always hating putting people out on strike as he said, 'Regardless of what you gain you never make up the money you lose.'

George Walden's office secretary, for the Northamptonshire Branch of the TGWU, was Mrs Warren. When she retired every bus passing her office tooted its horn in appreciation for her work. The AUEW local office was above Adams's cake shop in Mercers Row, Northampton, which was about 5 minutes walk from the Central Works.

Norman's work was 5½ days a week, reducing to Monday to Friday only, with call-outs when required.

One day he was called upon to go in on a Saturday as many buses had been damaged by storms and tree branches the night before. Jock Mitchell and 'Johnny' Johnson were ringing doorbells to get the Body Shop staff in to work, telephones not being as common then as nowadays. Norman was still in bed at the time.

Norman and Peter Gleave worked on one vehicle to make it an open-topper for the Wildlife Park at Woburn. Denise can remember that Peter and her father made a great team, and regularly wound up each other and the rest of the Works! On one occasion Peter was making new cage bottoms from offcuts for his birdcages, when Norman found them and hid them for a week. Peter then reproduced a new set. As he finished, the original set miraculously appeared back on his bench. Peter was not amused.

Denise remembers that her father was always available for work. Even when he was coming back from holiday in Eastbourne, the coach had a problem with a side locker. Norman was asked by the driver to repair it, which he did, dressed in his best suit. All United Counties staff and families travelled on the buses and coaches free, but dogs were charged at 10 shillings for a return ticket.

Denise remembers some of the children belonging to the workers, including those of Peter Gleave, Bill Horwood, Terry Dyson and 'Pongo 1' (Ron Faulkner), whose son Clive was called 'Pongo 2' when he worked at the Central Works. 'Tich' Hawes was Wilfred Hans Hawes, who in his spare time repaired everyone's watches and clocks.

One of the office workers was called Des O'Connor, whose mother lived near the County Cricket Ground in Northampton. Norah Parker used to work in the Wages Office at Derngate. Others that Denise remembers were Jeff Stainwright, Jim Foreman, Gordon Heard and 'Pop' Mayo. She can also remember the wedding of Terry and Doreen Dyson.

Norman got into bother with the

In the Body Shop are Clive Faulkner, Peter Gleave and Norman Abbott. *Denise Abbott collection*

police one year when he went scrumping for apples in the Northampton General Hospital orchard next door to the Works. He was caught and given a caution.

One day a bullock escaped from the slaughterhouse nearby and went through some of the hospital grounds. It fell through the bike sheds and crushed a couple of bikes, one belonging to Peter Gleave. The animal then tried to enter a bus via the rear passenger entrance and Norman met it trying to go up the stairs as he was coming down them.

On some Saturday mornings Denise used to go to the Works with her mother to pick up her father. They sometimes had to wait while Norman finished his shift then all went home to Castle Ashby together. She can remember many of the staff in the Works, and when she could drive she used to go in and take orders for fruit and vegetables, which she fetched from a farm at Billing. Denise parked her car in the Works car park while she worked at the Scottish & Newcastle building along Bedford Road.

United Counties used to do work for other NBC companies and in the late 1970s a fleet of white coaches came to Northampton for the new National Travel services. Later a

Bendi-Bus appeared in Northampton, but United Counties did not buy any.

In 1985/86 the Central Works was privatised and became known as United Counties Engineering. The secretarial department was also privatised. John Tate stressed in his letter that this move should not affect the rights of the individual. Apparently the bidding process was protracted, due to complaints from participating bidders.

By 1987 the basic skilled man was earning £151 for a 39-hour week with extras for overtime and weekend work. Holiday entitlement was 25 days a year. Wages were paid directly into bank accounts. Tea breaks were discontinued and so were bus passes. All staff had to record details of the job, times and non-stores-supplied items necessary for accurate costing and customer advice. Staff had to wash up in their own time, but tools could be put away in work time. They

Norman and Graham Roberts work on the air-conditioning units for the Leyland Tigers in the background. Denise remembers the scoops that Norman made for these coaches. *Denise Abbott collection*

were docked pay if late. There used to be 4 minutes grace, but this stopped. No incoming calls were allowed on the payphone, which had a light on the top that flashed when it rang; this was because the noise in the workshop could be quite loud. No staff were allowed to buy from Snap-On tool supplies on the premises. Insurance salesmen were also not permitted on United Counties premises.

United Counties staff ran a Staff Welfare Society, and in 1985 there were more than 400 members; 90 had benefited from the Society and 12 had received hardship payments. The Society also helped seven members who were in dispute with the company. The Society Secretary was K. Kidson and other committee members included Fred Moore, Peter Clack, J. Patrick, M. Coughlan and W. Whitaker.

Denise remembers that when a member of staff was getting married, his or her workbench was 'dressed' to celebrate the occasion. Here is one such occasion. *Denise Abbott collection*

Socially there were many clubs and societies at the Bedford Road site. Norman belonged to the Skittles club, and one match was against his late father's Castle Ashby team at Castle Ashby. This was a social event not just for the skittles, but the local barber came and cut the team's hair, being watched by Norman's mother's cat. Norman actually played for the home team that night. In 1974 Norman was the winner of a cash prize for the highest individual score in any round in a knockout skittles competition.

Castle Ashby House in 1981, with '60th Anniversary' buses in attendance. *Angela Seelig collection*

The Social Club also used to organise trips using United Counties vehicles. Denise remembers one such trip in 1974, when two coaches went down to London and the Royal Tournament. This particular show was

The 1975 United Counties raft team of Captain Peter Rowlands with crew of Les Porter, M. Watts and B. Bellham. Other crew members were J. Markie and D. Gibbons. *NBC News*

'bus push' at Billing Aquadrome.

Norman used to make his own wine and share it with his work colleagues. It used to be quite strong and the others were curious until they found out that he had been lacing it with vodka.

He used to keep his own tool kit at work, and when the Works was closing down he took Denise's car to collect the tools. He was concentrating so much on what he had to bring home that he accidentally reversed her car towards one of the pits. It was about 6 inches away when Terry Dyson stopped Norman before it actually went down the pit.

VanCrown Engineering was made up of Eastern National Engineering and United Counties Engineering. When the company closed on 22 May 1990 the staff were owed salaries for April and May, to be paid at the end of May and June, or two weeks pay.

The Cunningham family

Stuart Cunningham was an apprentice at the Central Works in Northampton from 1978 to 1982. His brother, John, was also an apprentice from 1980 to 1984. Their father Walter Cunningham worked there from 1955 as a

attended by the Princess Royal.

Norman used to support other events. One such was a raft race from Blackwood Hodge to Billing Aquadrome, through Northampton. Norman's contribution was to keep up the spirits of the rowers by throwing them cans of beer while taking the mickey from the banks of the River Nene near the Britannia pub.

The Central Works team was also involved in making a model bus for Northampton Carnival. This was to advertise a new National Travel campaign using frogs, renamed as Beepers. Norman also supported the

The United Counties pedal-powered 'mini bus' in Northampton Carnival with its support crew and a Leyland Leopard as back-up. *Denise Abbott collection*

mechanic and part-time driver, while another John Cunningham worked in the Trim Shop from 1960, then went to work at Aston Martin. An uncle, Kenneth Brittain, worked on the running shift, married office lady Phyllis Perkins and started his own coach firm. Derrick and Brian Labrum both worked in the electrical department. Walter's apprenticeship was for seven years, and apprentices had to join the union.

As his father had worked at the Central Works, Jock Mitchell said that Stuart would be able to start at 16 without an interview. However, when John came to start he had to have an interview. Their father's friends were Ken Cross and Gordon Heard, who was a motorbike fan.

Stuart worked with gearbox men Jeff Stainwright and Tony Blunt, who would give him a job stripping down a box then putting it back together properly; they would help out with any queries. The team worked very hard in the morning, sometimes going out to lunch at a local pub and sobering up in the afternoon. Tony Blunt married Yvonne from the Works office; she was a very attractive lady who was admired by the apprentices.

Some staff at the Works used to help each other out by clocking in their mates, which would prevent the colleague from being fined for being late. When the gearbox team were late one afternoon they were carpeted by Dennis Ord. Geoff and Tony took the blame, while Stuart went off to sleep in a corner.

Stuart remembers fellow apprentice John Sankey, and father and son Tulley. Jim Foreman was the Shop Steward and worked on engines. Keith Snedker was a very methodical man; he worked on engine building

The Pump Room at the Central Works with the regular team on the left and an apprentice on the right. Radio 2 is trying to keep them sane. *Roger Warwick collection*

and would get the apprentices to do work on his car for beer money. Mick Duffy was also an apprentice, and another good mechanic was John Tipler. Other apprentices were known as Indy and Mohammed. One fitter was called 'Killer' because he was afraid of swans after being attacked by one on the riverbank.

The biggest sin an apprentice could commit was to borrow a tool and not put it back without cleaning it first. Most apprentices gradually bought their own kit; however, Stuart and John did not need to, as they had kit at home.

Stuart did not like his four-year college career very much, as he was bored with the lectures. However, he used to go to a local pub at lunchtime and help his fellow students with problems. The lecturer was a Mr Wilkinson, known as 'Walt'. Stuart did enjoy a visit to the Institute of Engineers at Sywell Airport, and made many good contacts there.

One day the mechanics were removing an engine, and had to call the electricians to disconnect the wires. This usually worked all right, but they would not come out straight away so the mechanics did all their work and left the engine hanging only by its wires. Eventually these broke and had to be repaired, making the job a lot longer.

The various teams had radios to keep them amused. The gearbox team listened to Radio 1, while the Pump Room team were Radio 2 fans. Apprentices

The stores team of Dennis Taylor, John Brook, Jenny Gibson, Fred Doughty and Dick Farey. *United Counties News*

used to come out for a burst of Radio 1 to keep them
going. The Pump Room team were Harvey and Jeff,
and at times they had extra work. For example, once
when the fairground came to Midsummer Meadow an
apprentice was sent over and returned with a pump for
overhaul. More beer money for the apprentice!

When Stuart went out for his road test he was
back in 10 minutes, as he was very nervous. After a cup
of tea he went out again and passed.

Northampton Depot and Works worked closely
together. One day Stuart should have been sent out on
a breakdown, but was very tired and Charlie said he
would go instead. Unfortunately he was killed while
filling the bus with fuel on the motorway.

Ken Brittain took over the depot of York Bros
in Bridge Street, Northampton, and ran coaches and
buses from there. Stuart's father's brother-in-law was
a blacksmith on the same site. One of his conductors
was Fred Doughty, who worked for United
Counties; Stuart drove and Fred was his
regular conductor. Brittain's Coaches was
later bought out by Country Lion, then
sold to Souls of Olney.

Later on Walter Cunningham bought
the boys a minibus and started them
out as Cunningham Coaches. However,
they wanted other work and worked for
other companies, including Northampton
Corporation Transport, the RAC and
Cosworth; at the time of writing both
are working at Cummings Engines in
Daventry.

Cyril and Terry Green

Cyril was a driver for United Counties at
Long Buckby, where two crews were based.
He often used to take his bus home at
night ready for work the next day.

The main route to West Haddon was via Long
Buckby – route 306 – and market-day buses went
from Long Buckby to Daventry via Ashby St
Ledgers – route 307. Northampton to Daventry via
Ravensthorpe was route 308.

When Cyril had to give up driving he went to
work in the stores at the Central Works until he
retired.

Terry Green spent more than 25 years at the
Central Works. He started as an apprentice and moved
on to do fitting, worked in the Machine Shop and as a
welder. Central Works used to paint all buses by hand,
and made and repaired their own seats.

Terry remembers that some staff used waste test
engine oil to keep their cars going as it was good, but
had to be disposed of by the company. Most of it went
to Duston Laundry, where it was burned.

Keith Snedker

Keith started working at the Central Works in 1950
as an apprentice, aged 15. His training was gained by
working with trained men in each department; after
six years he qualified and specialised in engine repairs
and rebuilds. Later in his career Keith used to train
up the new apprentices under the training scheme
organised by the Training Manager, Jim Foreman;
he felt that this scheme was one of the best in the
National Bus Company.

Keith became one of the four AUEW shop
stewards in the Central Works. He was not a
confrontational unionist, but preferred to use his
negotiating skills when needed. He would only fight
if he knew he could get a result. If management had
already decided on an outcome, it was not worth trying
to change their minds.

**Two of Keith's colleagues in the repair bays at the
Central Works.** *Roger Warwick collection*

In the early years of his union work Keith found
out that second-hand sales of vehicles were dealt with
by gentlemen's agreements. Some dealers made good
profits out of re-sales, many of the vehicles going to
Africa and Hong Kong. Keith helped to get one back
working when he was over there on holiday.

One part of Keith's work involved the use of
a company car to visit depots and help to sort out
problems with the engines. Socially he became
involved in the skittles team and refereed some
football matches.

Keith left United Counties with a redundancy
package when Stagecoach took over. He has since
worked for a few companies, including a period with
Northampton Corporation Buses, now part of the
First Group.

Brian Rogers

Brian spent 38 years painting buses for United Counties. He started in September 1951 as an apprentice, which lasted six years, including day release to Northampton Technical College in St George's Avenue, where he learned the art of signwriting, an art he only used in his last few years of painting buses

When his apprenticeship was completed, Brian did two years of National Service in the Northamptonshire Regiment, being trained at Wootton Barracks, followed by Donniford Camp at Watchet in Somerset, then a tour in Aden. After Aden Brian returned to the United Counties Works and stayed there until he was made redundant in 1990.

Brian cycled to work every day until he bought a car. He had a bus pass but it was easier and quicker to cycle.

Brian remembers that the buses used to have transfer fleet numbers applied before metal plates were used. One of his early jobs was to stick these on and varnish them. When metal plates were used they arrived made up with a black base coat. The colour they were painted was determined by the depot to which each bus was going.

The colouring was:

Northampton	Green
Stony Stratford	Green with black left and right edges
Wellingborough	Red

Rushden	Red with black left and right edges
Bedford	Blue
Biggleswade	Blue with black left and right edges
Huntingdon	Blue with yellow left and right edges
Aylesbury	Blue with red left and right edges
Kettering	Yellow
Corby	Yellow with black left and right edges
Stamford	Yellow with red left and right edges
Luton	Brown
Hitchin	Brown with black left and right edges

In the early days a Mr Metcalfe used to be subcontracted to come and do any signwriting on United Counties buses, which may have included some of the advertisements.

All Brian's painting was by hand brush. Later on some buses were spray painted, which was done at the Bedford Depot Paint Shop. In recent times this shop has reverted to hand-painting.

Some adverts were painted on and others were on paper, being pasted on, sized then varnished over to make them weatherproof. Internal adverts were also pasted on and varnished.

A 25 years service party in 1976. The back row includes, from the left, Tom Smith, Don Hickerson, Ray Needle, Stan Palmer, Fred Pack, John Tate, Ray Burdett, Ken Clegg, Peter Gleave and Dick Fenton. The front row includes, from the left, Bert Brown, George Millen, Freddy Dark, Brian Rogers (second from right) and Keith Snedker. *Brian Rogers collection*

Unusually, on some of the Lodekkas illuminated advert boxes were used on one side; the adverts were stuck onto the back of the Perspex, which had been removed. Of course, the adverts had to be the wrong way round when pasted on, to be the right way round when seen by the public. However, the heat from the lights used to make the paper curl.

Unusual painting jobs included an advert for Chiltern Radio. The paint team have also been called upon to paint vehicles on a contract basis for preservationists; one of these was a former London Transport bus.

When Brian started, each bus would be varnished after painting. As a result, three buses were painted each week.

Later on varnishing was abolished and four buses were painted at the same time.

Originally the buses were painted Tilling Green and Tilling Cream, the colours varying slightly with the manufacturer; those used included Dulux and Parsons. Later, National Bus Company green and white were used. At deregulation, buses became a darker green with orange stripes, and later still were painted in Stagecoach house colours of white with

A 30 years service party in 1981. In the back, third from the left, is Mick Berry, and Brian is fourth from the left. *Brian Rogers collection*

orange, red and blue stripes.

When a bus was being repainted, 50% undercoat and 50% topcoat was applied first on any new panels, then a topcoat. Otherwise, only a topcoat was used. All were varnished if specified. If a bus had been rebuilt, a grey primer may have been used first.

For a few years, while ventilation systems were being applied to coaches at the Central Works, the painters were bussed to Milton Keynes in their own blue-painted bus. As it was not a service bus, some of the drivers had passed driving exams for United Counties engineers only. The facility at Milton Keynes was clean and spacious, but the team were glad when they returned to Northampton. From these days Brian remembers that the body man at Milton Keynes was called Conrad

Brian hard at work smoothing out a stick-on transfer on a National coach at Milton Keynes Depot in March 1985. *Conrad Winchcombe, Brian Rogers collection*

Winchcombe. Buses and coaches were being painted in National colours in those days.

Brian remembers that some of the older road staff would come to the Works to finish off their time before retiring. They were called the 'brush hands' and they used to paint the undercoats and rub them down and paint and varnish the insides. Only the regular painters were allowed to paint the top coats. As part of their job, the 'brush hands' would paint and varnish the stairs and the seat frames. The window sills were stained with a home-produced concoction.

When Brian started there were ten people working in the Paint Shop, which was next door to the Body Shop and had an entrance to the back yard of the Works. Brian remembers some of the painters with whom he worked during his 38 years: Jack Craddock, Jack Wright, Eric Fincher, Tony Collins, Jock Selby, Harry Mcatter, Tony Osborne, Alf Aldsworth (signwriter), Dennis Burbage, Clive Ashton, Wilf Surridge, Francis Ward, Fred Darley, Ted Underwood, Peter Billson, Jack Chambers, Bill Rollings, Cliff Rappitt, Fred Adams, Dave Croucher, Cyril Care, Roy Muscutt, Fred Minney, Aubrey Wykes, Len Catlin, Eddie Eglis, Len Timms, Alf Sale, Ted Stenson, Norman Stratton, Bill Chambers, Fred Townsend, Ted Tranter, Ron Wykes, Albert Plowman, Keith David,

One of the four 1921-1981 Anniversary buses with the painting team. From left to right they are Mick Crane, Keith David, Alf Aldsworth (who did the signwriting), Bill Horwood, Sid Thurston, Brian Rogers, Clive Ashton, Len Timms, Eddie Eglis, Cliff Rappitt and Dave Croucher. *Brian Rogers and Steve Loveridge collections*

Bill Blacknell, Mervyn Crawford, Sid Thurston, Peter Tebbutt, Bert Humphreys, Walt Burks, Roy Clark, Bill Burt, Martin Judd, Mick Crane, Bryan Walter, Sid Metcalfe (signwriter), Ernie Short, Taff Chambers, Paddy Delaney and Sylvia Allen. He also remembers fitter Brian Ward, Martin Lloyd from the office, and Rance Muscutt.

Some of his colleagues used unusual words when talking – one said that he was going home to clean his 'varicle' (vehicle).

After 1990 and until he retired Brian was a painter and decorator. The only alternative was working at Wolverton Carriage Works, but that meant leaving home at 5.00am every day to catch a train and walk to work.

When United Counties Engineering was privatised it had its own livery, shown on the lorry to the right. The company had a contract to paint United Counties Coachlinks vehicles, and here is one with its proud painters, Alf Aldsworth, Clive Ashton, Eddie Eglis and Brian Rogers. *Brian Rogers collection*

Jeff Stainwright

Jeff was born in London and on leaving school he applied to work in the Civil Service at Whitehall. Taking a year to be approved, he worked at various temporary jobs, one of which was working in the London County Council Film Library. He then worked for the Post Office Engineering Department from 1959 to 1968, when his father was transferred to rural Wellingborough to work for a company on the Denington Industrial Estate.

Being bound by the Official Secrets Act, Jeff was not able to speak about this work, but remembers one incident vividly. He was called to a government building to mend a printing machine, which was jammed; the paper had to be extracted for disposal, and the bits were pieced together to make sure they were all there. When the staff were happy, Jeff was asked to take the bag of bits down to the boiler room

and make sure they were incinerated, which he and a member of staff did. On the floor of the boiler room were many magazines and old papers; Jeff was glancing through this pile and found a brown envelope addressed to a prominent MP. This envelope was open and inside was a copy of the Communist Newspaper. This may sound quite harmless to outsiders, but it caused mass hysteria in this Civil Service Department, as at that time Harold Wilson's Labour Party was, in some circles, thought to be a little too left wing ('reds under the beds'). The staff member called up the security service and he and Jeff were cross-questioned about the incident. Jeff felt as though he was being tried for treason at least, but it was all quite innocent. Apparently, the MP was questioned about the matter but Jeff does not know what happened to him.

Jeff was a postman for a short while, but did not like the job and applied to United Counties, being taken on at the Central Works in 1969. For the next 20 years Jeff specialised in overhauling and repairing gearboxes. He started as a semi-skilled fitter, as he had had some experience in working on cars before joining the company, skills that he found were easily transferable to the bus industry. However, after four weeks he applied for a skilled fitter's pay, and this was granted.

Living in Wellingborough, Jeff went to work on the bus. He started at 7.30am, and the bus used to drop off him and his colleagues by Northampton

Hospital. Even with running the short distance to the works, they still arrived at 7.32am, which meant that they had 15 minutes docked from their pay for being late. The bus crews were urged to get the staff there on time, but could not always make it happen. For some reason, the clocks at the Central Works were always 4 minutes ahead of British Summer or Greenwich Mean Time, so even if you thought you were early, by company time you were, in fact, late.

Central Works had five pits, engine overhaul bays, pump shop,

gearbox bays and Body Shop, and upstairs was the Trimming Shop. Jeff learned to drive a forklift truck. One day he lifted a mate up outside the first floor window of the Trimming Shop, who then knocked the window and waved in. This scared the trimmers and they were amazed as the figure was gradually lowered out of sight, waving as he went.

Many staff at Bedford Road met their partners there and also had ongoing affairs. Certain staff were known for their affairs, and they used to play tricks on each other; unfortunately, most of these cannot be reproduced in this book.

Jeff started working with Ollie Collins. Ollie had worked for United Counties since 1946, so his knowledge of gearboxes was good. He used to shout at everybody, and some staff were too frightened to work with him for this reason. One of these was Bill Derby. Jeff, however, asked to work with Ollie. Ollie specialised in the semi-automatic gearboxes, while Jeff

looked after the manual boxes. At the Central Works new boys used to work with an old hand and learn the tricks of the trade.

The works was a closed shop union-wise and Jeff was told he had to join the AUEW. However, he did not agree with their policies and joined the TGWU instead. He worked closely with Jim Foreman in later years, and got on well with him, despite the fact that he was an AUEW steward. The unions were very strong and each team was only allowed to do work relating to their trade – mechanics, electricians, bodybuilders, etc – and there were demarcation lines that had to be adhered to. Jeff got into trouble one day for removing two wires from a gearbox to get on with his own work, because the bus was needed back in service in a hurry. He was told that he had broken all union agreements and had to replace the two wires himself, as he had taken them off. He found this petty, and refused to deal with the union members. The funny thing was, however, that when out at a breakdown and an electrical fault had occurred, Jeff was allowed to mend that without union disapproval.

Talking of breakdowns, Jeff was flexible to go out on breakdowns and do repairs at little notice; he needed the extra money to buy a house and was

In later years some of the all-over advertisements were entirely done using transfers. Here are a couple of National Holidays examples. *Both Brian Rogers collection*

From the Painting Department archive: two VRs, one for Milton Keynes Citybus and one for United Counties, a National single-decker, and a Heathrow express coach. *All Brian Rogers collection*

Part of the Central Works with Chief Engineer Charles Blomfield and three officials from Northampton Borough Council touring the works. *Roger Warwick collection*

prepared to work long hours to achieve this. He used to enjoy the challenge of solving a problem and getting the bus back on the road.

On one occasion Jeff and a colleague were sent to Derngate to repair a Royal Blue coach that had broken down. No replacement vehicle was available, so they had to work quickly to find the problem, lying under the bus and working without a pit. The driver and passengers were entertained to tea and biscuits in the canteen while they worked.

On another occasion, a United Counties coach broke down in Bath. Jeff was sent down to mend it and had to work in the mud in a corner of the yard at the bus garage, as the workshop was busy with its own buses. United Counties sent out the Northampton breakdown truck, but it broke down. The Kettering breakdown truck was being repaired, which had to be completed before it could be sent to rescue its Northampton counterpart. Once this was done, it was sent down to collect Jeff and the coach. All this

took three days in total. Jeff was also once sent to Leighton Buzzard to repair a gearbox, in a shed with no facilities, and had to lie on the ground again to do the job.

Over the years United Counties had many breakdown trucks. The best one, Jeff remembers, was the AEC Matador, which Jeff always thought was illegal, as the headlights were too high off the road. However, it could pull or lift any vehicle. The Foden and the early 1931 Leyland former bus were also very reliable. The Foden's gearbox was rebuilt by Jeff. It was stripped and a list made of the parts needed. Due to the truck being very old, no parts books were available and Jeff was sent to Foden's factory in Sandbach, Cheshire, with a blank cheque for the parts needed. The old parts were deposited on the counter and the Foden storesmen went out of their way and found enough new parts for Jeff to rebuild the gearbox.

Not long after this rebuild, the old 1931 Leyland half-cab breakdown truck gearbox gave up, being more than 40 years old at the time. Jock Mitchell found an old gearbox, and the two of them fixed it up to give the truck a few more years of work. Jeff also changed the head gaskets on the Matador, a job that lasted nearly all day.

United Counties bought a couple of Ford chassis

and did them up for breakdown vehicles. The problem with these D Series former tippers was that they were not heavy enough for lifting double-decker buses with front engines. This meant that every time they went to lift a bus, the lorry's front wheels came off the ground. The Fords were only used for towing and were thus a waste of money really.

Jeff was taught to drive a bus and was passed out by Norman Redhead early in his bus career, in 1970. John Appleton was working with Norman at this time. Jeff passed his PSV (now PCV) Licence in 1973.

The most difficult bus that Jeff drove was a 1920s former RAF Leyland bus owed by Mike Sutcliffe at Dunstable. A similar Leyland Charabus was partly restored as a special project by apprentice Neil Wilmin, Jeff and other specialists, in their 'spare' time. The bus had a top speed of about 20mph, but Jeff would only drive it at 12mph due to the virtual non-existent braking capacity. He only drove it for 20 minutes, and had to yank the steering wheel round 1½ times for a full lock to go round corners. He nearly hit a car, whose driver pulled in front, then slowed right down so that his children could see the old bus. The emergency stop was avoided, as Jeff indicated to the car driver to get out of the way.

At times of peak work, Gardner engine overhauls were farmed out to Brookside Motors of Wellingborough. One of Jeff's tasks was to take a bus home at night and drop it at Brookside, pick up an overhauled bus and take it to Wellingborough Garage overnight, then take it back to work next day. Sometimes his work colleagues would catch a lift back home, leaving work early to do so. An occasional problem with these overhauls was that the engine timing was not correctly done. This meant that the bus was slow to go up hills, and had to be taken into the Central Works for adjustment.

When Ollie left, Jeff took charge of his section; he used to train the apprentices and had a regular mate to work with. Some of the apprentices were very good listeners and would learn quickly, some would take a bit more time to learn the skills, and others were hopeless. One of the better ones let himself down by wearing a cap to college and refusing to take it off. He was taken to the Works Manager, who told him off. Jeff remembers that he trained Paul Grimes, whose father Peter was a manager at United Counties. Peter later went on to be a director with Luton & District buses. Paul Woolmore was another of the apprentices trained by Jeff. Sometimes Jeff would train two apprentices together. Terry Green worked as a lathe operator, as did Dennis Allen, both being skilled machinists. Jeff remembers apprentices Graham Neal and Jim York (son of the owner of York Bros coaches at Cogenhoe). He remembers father and son Taffy and Mick Watts, and John and John Tulley, again father and son. He remembers a Mr Ratley, who had been a prisoner of war, and Mr and Mrs Rusky, who

were cleaners. Mr Rowland was a bodyman, and Andy Patenall had a very unfortunate accident after leaving United Counties, when his fingers were chopped off by a flywheel falling on them. Jeff found that many staff had family also working in the company; he worked with Mark Mitchell, who was the grandson of Jock Mitchell (the Works Superintendent).

Jeff had one serious accident while at United Counties. He and an apprentice were sent out to Aylesbury to do a job, which was tricky and the apprentice had not been much use, so Jeff was exhausted. He therefore asked the apprentice to drive home. They were in the company Morris Minor van at the time and the apprentice went into a trance and nearly hit a Land Rover coming the other way. Jeff grabbed the wheel and diverted the van, which swerved and went through a hedge and up-ended in a water-filled ditch. The apprentice was unhurt but Jeff spent several days in Aylesbury Hospital and several weeks recovering from a broken wrist. The apprentice moved sections after that, and Jock Mitchell and Stan Simons went out to sort out the problem.

Jimmy Bowden and Taffy Watts used to drive the stores lorries. Jeff and his team also worked on these vehicles. One of Jeff's mates was Tony Blunt, who came as the best apprentice and wanted to work on gearboxes. There were two apprentices called Martin Brown. Unfortunately, the one from Wellingborough was killed in a motorcycle accident, and a result his father donated a cup, which was given to the best United Counties apprentice each year.

Bill Law used to overhaul and repair the company car fleet. One day he made a joke at a manager's expense. He was being asked to do about five jobs at once and said that he did not have time to do them as he was going into hospital next day. The manager was upset that he had not been told, and asked who would do all the work. Never mind, was the reply, I am going in to have another pair of hands fitted so that I can do all these jobs at once. The manager was not impressed and stormed off. Jeff remembers Mr Law for his wit, and was saddened when he had a blackout, fell down his stairs and died at the age of 70. He looked out for Mrs Law until she died a couple of years before this book was written.

The company cars were run into the ground in a short period of time. However, staff were able to buy them at knock-down prices and do them up for a lot less than buying a new or second-hand one. Therefore most of them found new homes, sometimes the work being done before they left the Central Works. Jeff bought a Morris Marina, which lasted for quite a few years before he got rid of it. Having given up the bus travel, Jeff was travelling to work by car now, with a company parking pass.

After a year or so the new semi-automatic-gearbox Bristol RELH coaches started to play up. The first of these was numbered 270, which ran for more than a million miles for United Counties. This gearbox was a 'one-off', being fitted with an eight-holed input flange and matching input shaft from the fluid clutch to the gearbox. The fluid clutch was also a 'one-off'; Jeff came across only two others of this type in 28 years working with bus gearboxes. The bellows-type gland fitted into a recess in the aluminium casing, similar to the type fitted to the RELL fluid flywheels; however, that type was not recessed.

RELH coach 282, based at Hitchin, was the other vehicle in the fleet fitted with a recessed fluid clutch, which was fitted with the standard four-hole (smaller) flange. Both these coaches had to have their clutch units rebuilt and returned or repaired and fitted by Jeff, as no spare units were available. As these fluid clutches were of different dimensions from the standard type (Llewellyn gland), the input shaft was longer, which was also to cause problems when they became due for replacement or repair. As an afterthought, Jeff

Jeff looks on as apprentice Ian Wilson works on a gearbox. *Colin Clubb collection*

remembers that when the early Bristol REs were being de-licensed, Northampton stores found a box of bits containing some of the parts for converting 270 to a standard-gearbox coach.

This and the other semi-automatic work kept Ollie and later Jeff going full-time as more and more vehicles had gearboxes of this type. Examples of the vehicles were the coaches, Bristol RELL buses, Bristol VR double-deckers and, later, Leyland Nationals and Leyland Leopards. The Leyland Tiger coaches and Olympian buses had hydrocyclic gearboxes.

Jeff worked under many managers. However, he remembers that Mr George Sell would not speak directly to him. When called into the office, Gordon Heard, the Foreman in charge of Jeff's section, had to go too. George would talk to Gordon and Gordon would have to relay the message to Jeff – it was all to do with rank in the company. Many of the managers had been officers in the Army and carried this hierarchy through into civilian life.

Howard 'Johnny' Johnson was different. He would call Jeff 'my boy' and would ask him to do all sorts of unusual engineering tasks, as he knew Jeff would do his best. One day Jeff and his mate were sent off to Luton depot to mend a bus. 'Johnny' expected it to take a long time, but a few hours after being sent they were back having done the job. Jeff was congratulated for the quick work and sent home early.

The Driving Instructors used to keep a 'Black Museum' of damaged bus engine and gearbox parts, to show new and bad drivers the damage they could and had done. Drivers were brought to the gearbox section to see how automatic transmissions worked, and

watched as gearboxes were run on the test rig.

United Counties buses had a full general overhaul initially every seven years, and Mick Berry was in charge of them. This involved a complete strip-down and replacement of all worn parts and refurbishment of other parts. Overhauls stopped in the 1970s and major docks became the normal procedure. New spare parts were at a premium, due to the three-day working week and industrial disputes at suppliers. Jeff might order six parts from the stores next door and be given one, as that was all that was available. He would then have to make the replacements or do up one from one of the scrapped gearboxes kept in the yard outside. Ken Cross used to grind cranks to reuse them. Except in problem cases, all buses would be back on the road in a week after coming into the works. Jeff and his mate could remove a gearbox in a Bristol VR in 3 hours, repair it and put it back the same day, or early the next day.

To help his job specialist tools were needed. In the early years Jeff would ask for a new tool and be told to make it himself, as the company would not buy it. This could be a false economy, however, as it would take up to three days to design and make, and many gearboxes could have been repaired in that time, had the tool been bought off the shelf that day.

TBD 278G was a Bristol RELH coach at Wellingborough Depot. It was sent to the works for repair and was in a hell of a mess. Others of the class had needed spares, and the Depot Engineer, Les King, had robbed this bus of spares to keep others on the road. The engine and gearbox were missing, as were other vital parts. Jeff was put to work to find the missing gearbox parts, the EP valve, all the pipework, brackets, clips, speedo, fluid clutch, fitting bolts, specialised nuts and unions, etc. While making the list and sorting part numbers, Keith Snedker asked Jeff to fit and pressure-test a fluid flywheel on an engine he had built and tested, and which had to go to a depot urgently. When Keith saw the state of the vehicle Jeff was working on, he christened 278 'Stainwright's Dilemma'. With the main works expertise and skill, the vehicle was back on the road. Incidentally this bus is, at the time of writing, about 30 years later, going through another overhaul at Express Motors in North Wales, for reuse there. An old damaged body panel from this bus was used by Jeff to repair his wife's Morris Minor – a bit of rubbing down and a repaint and you wouldn't know the difference! He still owns the car today.

Talking of Morris Minors, a Traveller was restored in the works for one of the managers, being given a thorough overhaul and MOT before going out on the road. The MOTs were done in a special bay in Northampton Depot running repair workshop, next door to the Central Works. United Counties employed their own MOT staff and used to do MOTs for anyone who would pay them to do so.

At times of vehicle shortages, United Counties would buy in old vehicles from other NBC companies. In one case a few vehicles arrived from the Isle of Wight. They were 20 years old, but had only been used in the summer and stored in the winter, so were only about 10 years old in bus terms. They were unusual in that they had a 12-volt power supply instead of the usual 24 volts on United Counties buses. However, several parts disappeared off these buses and were used to repair cars belonging to various employees. Some of the bought-in former Red & White 1950s Bristol LS single-decker buses were strange as the fuel tanks were on the wrong side, which meant that they had to go through fuel bays the wrong way round, which caused problems at peak times at depots.

The worst problems encountered by the Central Works were with the former Luton Corporation buses. These were in such a bad state that vast sums of money were spent just to get them through an MOT. One arrived with a canvas body panel, which had to be replaced.

One of Jeff's favourite buses was the K type. He remembers that the oldest in the fleet was 911, which was converted into a driver trainer. He also remembers that preserved 964 was the 'pet' bus at Wellingborough. It outlived all the others of its type there and was kept pristine. It was only supposed to work on town services, but one day found itself at Derngate. It was seen by management and Wellingborough was told off for sending such an old vehicle to Northampton when it should have sent a newer vehicle. However, 964 had been sent due to a spares shortage for more modern buses, and was the only one available.

When Derngate Bus Station closed the building was used as a grain store by a local grain merchant. Jeff's father-in-law was in charge of a mill that processed a good percentage of the Derngate grain.

Jeff remembers that in later years the five-speed gearboxes were taken out of the old Bristol Lodekka vehicles, modified and fitted into the BVW-engined Bristol FLF 70-seater buses. This was due to the difficulty in obtaining spare parts for the Bristol BVW engines, whereas the Gardner engines were 'two a penny'. Most of the LDs were completely stripped of engines, gearboxes and other reusable parts before going to the scrapyard at Barnsley. They therefore all had to be towed up by breakdown lorry. Parts for Bristol engines were so scarce that Volvo pistons were bought and adapted to replace worn-out examples, but Jeff is not sure whether this was successful.

Another job that the team had to do in the 1960s was to replace the air bags in Bristol FS buses with coil springs. These were harder wearing and did not frighten the customers when they broke. Apparently more than one pensioner thought she had been shot when the air bag burst with a loud bang. Jeff worked with Mick Berry when he first started, and was told this tale, which amused him.

Jeff and his mate used to be called on to help other departments at peak times. The unions were not so strong in later years, so they became used to doing any job that needed doing, which was a change from their normal speciality work.

Each bus used to have a Maintenance Card, which recorded its full history from the time of its purchase until its sale. The total mileage was the sum of the route distances the bus did, as the early buses did not have odometers. This was a useful means of highlighting a problem bus and trying to solve the problems before the bus broke down.

One charity event that Jeff remembers was the 'bus push' round Billing Aquadrome in April 1977. An old former Lincolnshire Bristol SC was delivered from a scrap merchant and adapted for the push by having grab rails attached to its sides. The Ministry man would not allow it to be driven to Billing so it had to be towed by breakdown lorry, and he was there to make sure that it was not driven. The push went well and after 28 hours a large cheque for £1,500 was sent to a charity, which made it all worth while. Organised by Martin Lloyd, the event was attended by Company Chairman Freddy Wood.

Jeff and the other staff were asked to provide constructive suggestions to improve the company. More than 600 entries were submitted, including some from Jeff. Several of the works staff were included in a photograph for the company newsletter accompanying an article on this scheme, which was known as 'QED'.

Central Works had more than 100 employees at its peak, but also had other residents. These were the rats that lived there, and the mice that used to run over the

roof girders. One of Jeff's mates threw an engine part at one once; it made a mess of the part but the rat ran away unharmed.

Jeff once had to go to Battersea Wharf, London, late at night, to tow a coach back to Northampton. Before he could do so he had to evict the 'gentlemen of the road' who had settled down for a good night's sleep in relative comfort. They were not happy to be evicted and their night disturbed.

Jeff remembers one funny incident that involved the running shift fitter, Freddy Raggett. He was asked to take a Bristol SU vehicle up to Derngate Bus Station and park it on a particular bay ready for service. He did as he was asked, then went into town for lunch. The rostered bus driver got into the bus and tried to start it without success. The shift fitter on duty was sent up in the van to sort out the problem. He went to check the fuel tank and found a hole where the filler neck should have been. He then looked under the bus and found there was no fuel tank there at all. Freddy had accidentally taken the wrong SU; the one he should have taken was parked next to it. The bus had got up to Derngate using up the fuel in the filter and pump. This incident resulted in red faces all round and a breakdown truck to take the bus back to the depot for a replacement tank.

Ready to go: Len Flattery is in the trilby, while Jeff and Ray Mace push on the other side. *Jeff Stainwright collection*

Martin Lloyd and Freddy Wood celebrate after the 28-hour charity 'bus push' with some of the other 100 pushers at Billing Aquadrome in 1977. Between Martin and Freddy are Jeff Smith, Peter Mace, Martin Worrall and Ray Mace. Paul Woolmore is hiding in the right background with the dark glasses, and Jill Faulkener is the second woman from the left at the bottom of photograph. Other pushers included Colin Clubb, Michael Carr, Steve Mace, Jeff Stainwright, Len Flattery, Clive Smith, Dave Croucher, Steve Bass, Clive Faulkner, Steve Chamberlain, Phil Bliss, Bob Stafford, Keith David, Ron Galvin, Geoff Putnam and Peter Rowlands. *NBC News*

In later years Jeff became a bit disillusioned with the works. When he started the old boys used to have a good, quiet job, they did it well and no one interfered with them. The younger lads used to do the other dirtier jobs and sweep the floor. However, Jeff found when he was an 'old boy' he was still doing the dirty jobs, and the cleaner jobs were being done by the youngsters, because they refused to do the dirty ones, which he considered was not right.

When United Counties was deregulated in 1988, redundancies were handed out to some staff, and the company was split up into four units for sale: United Counties, Milton Keynes, Luton & District, and the Works, which became United Counties Engineering (UCE).

Jeff had been approached by Luton & District to work for them. He could not see much of a future for UCE, so decided to leave. After much negotiating and setting of terms and conditions suitable to both parties, he set up an independent Transmission Section for the company, called Luton & District Transmissions. It lasted for eight years before Jeff moved to Cosworth Engineering in Wellingborough, where he was building and testing Rolls Royce engines until the contract finished two years later. Jeff then drove lorries and vans, finally driving a bus for disabled children to and from school.

Jeff retired early and now restores old cars and military vehicles for himself and others. He has

Some of the Central Works 'QED' team, including at the back 'Roland Rat' and Alan Hall. On the front row, second from left is Tommy Kerr, fourth from left is Ken Halford, hiding behind Mark Mitchell is Keith Snedker, and second from the right is Jeff Stainwright. *NBC News*

also done some contracting work on gearboxes and grinding brake drums (40 a day) for other companies. His hobby now is finding, restoring and repairing old clocks.

Neil Wilmin

Neil lived in Grendon and went to school in Wollaston. His first brush with the bus industry was while he was still at school, when he had a part-time job working in the gardens belonging to Mr Bob York who owned York Bros coaches of Cogenhoe.

Ever since he can remember, Neil has taken things apart and put them together again. It started with his toys and gradually moved on to motorbikes, then cars. He learned this from his father, who used to do the same.

On leaving school in 1983, Neil applied for an apprenticeship at United Counties. He had a rigorous interview at Bedford Road with a panel including Jim Foreman, the training officer.

The company took on about six new apprentices a year. Some were based at local depots and others, like Neil, were based at the main works. Four days were spent in the works and initially one day a week at Wellingborough Technical College. Wellingborough was the base for all United Counties apprentices, who worked with apprentices from other local transport firms.

The apprenticeship lasted just over four years, which included times of block release at college. The college work was mainly on lorries, but the techniques were similar to buses. The first three months consisted

of an intensive basic mechanics course with Jim Foreman. He showed them the tools they would need and how to use them. This included learning how to drill a hole and tap it to hold a stub-bolt. After this training, all apprentices worked with skilled men for a minimum of two years, who taught them the various jobs. Departments in the works included Dock, Engine, Engine Head, Gearbox, Welders, Pumps, Axles, Body, Painters and Trimmers. For instance, two men would strip and rebuild an engine and ten engine bays were in use at any one time. Another man was employed to clean the engines before reassembly. All engine reboring was done at the works, and two men were kept busy on lathes.

Neil remembers that at one time an old Bristol RELL was painted two-tone blue and used to take painters to Winterhill Depot daily. The engine was sold out of the bus and the painters returned to Northampton. From those days Neil remembers Bob Smith, and other apprentices he got to know were Alan Bates, Robbie McKenzie, Keith Baldock at Stony Stratford and Rob Prested. He also remembers that Bob Slade was a skilled man. Other works staff included Ken Cross (Engineering Foreman), Jeff Stainwright, Brian Ward, Keith Gibbons, Colin Stockley, John Honey, Graham Neal and John Charlton.

Neil (right) with his project engine and fellow apprentice Del Merry. *Neil Wilmin collection*

One of Neil's projects was stripping and rebuilding an engine from an ancient Charabus, owned by Leyland man Mike Sutcliffe. This was a long project and caused problems, such as being unable to start it. Fortunately a jig was designed that helped with this task. The project lasted nine months.

Neil spent some time training at Kettering and Corby, and from those days he remembers John Storey, an electrician, and John Tipler.

Neil was taught to drive by Brian Barton at Kettering. He remembers that all the training buses used to congregate at one depot or another at lunchtime. Neil was tested by Tom Poulter, and he remembers Johnny Appleton as the Chief Instructor. From Rothersthorpe Avenue days he remembers Colin Stafford.

Neil won several awards while at United Counties. One of these was the Martin Brown Memorial Trophy for the best apprentice in his year. As mentioned above, the trophy had been presented to the company by Martin's father, in memory of his son, an apprentice who had been killed in a motorbike accident.

Neil went to Birmingham for a skills test and passed with 97%. He was then taken on by United Counties, and worked there for eight years before leaving for pastures new.

The works were made ready for privatisation by being reformed as United Counties Engineering (UCE) under Geoff Pullin. This became a franchise for ERF and Foden lorries, but this work was infrequent and the staff were bored. When UCE ceased trading, Neil was taken on by Stagecoach at Rothersthorpe Avenue Garage. He started on the shift system at Northampton Depot; the shifts worked were 5.00am-2.00pm and 2.00pm-midnight. There was also a day shift in the works from 7.30am to 4.30pm. United Counties apprentices were much sought after, and Northampton Transport used to poach the best ones when they qualified.

After leaving Stagecoach Neil worked at First Bus Northampton for five years, from where he remembers former United Counties man Bill Sye, then he went back to Stagecoach at Bedford, where he worked on the MOT section, MK Metro, Peter Clark Services,

Neil (left) with his trophy as the most successful heavy vehicle mechanic. George Fell (third from left) from Milton Keynes won the first Martin Brown Trophy as best United Counties student.

Later, Neil also won this trophy. Also included in the photograph are Divaker Patel, Len Warne, Terry Smith, Geoff Pullin and John Richards. *NBC News*

and now works at Arriva in Aylesbury. From his Bedford days he remembers that the Manager was Derek Irwin, and other staff included Malcolm Harris and Craig, the foreman.

Harvey William Brown

Harvey worked at the main works for 25 years, from 1962, aged 15, to 1986, when the works was closed. He was a member of the Allied Engineering Workers Union, becoming a shop steward. (Later the AUEW amalgamated with the TGWU, and has now become UNITE.) This was the happiest part of his working career. He went through the comprehensive United Counties five-year apprentice training scheme and became a fitter. He also worked on the running shift and standby shifts, where he worked in a team that dealt with all breakdowns locally and on the M1 motorway.

Harvey and his fellow union officials tried to get their members parity of wages and conditions with other engineering companies in the area. As a result they would negotiate hard with the management and sometimes hold strikes to put across their points more forcibly. These strikes sometimes included picketing the works, with only emergency work being done. During strikes the union officials, one of which was John Gibson, would make sure the staff got sixpence for being on strike –hopefully this was per hour, not per week.

One of these breakdown trucks was a converted Matador, which took ages to get anywhere at 35mph. One day Charlie Briggs and Harvey went to London and took a short cut through Hyde Park. When stopped by an official they were able to blind him with science and got away.

Charlie was the fitter who lost his life on the M1. He was in the incident with coach driver Roy Burdett, who was injured but recovered. Roy, Malcolm Cox and a colleague were delivering replacement coaches to Northampton when one ran out of fuel.

All works staff had to clock in and out, and Harvey's works number was 211. The running shift was on duty all day and night. One shift was 2.00pm Saturday to 2.00am Sunday, but if called out they might be not back at base until the early shift started on Monday morning. The late shift included fuelling up all the buses, checking the oil and water and occasionally sweeping them out. The best way to wash them was with the roof-mounted bus wash – down to wash, up to rinse. The modern programmed wash took three times as long to do the same thing.

The running shift always had four spare vehicles to replace breakdowns; some of these might have been in the Paint Shop or in the reserve fleet in the back yard. When economists started to run the business, spare buses were not kept.

The early shift fitter would start at 4.00am to unlock the depot and check the vehicles ready for the first workers' buses. The first out would be the 4.30am bus to Corby works, with 12 double-deckers going to Piano Forte works at Roade and many more going to British Timken at Duston.

Being at a similar height to the River Nene, across the Midsummer Meadow, the main works was built on stilts and rafts with water underneath. When the hole was dug for the new steam generator, the workers had to battle with their hole filling up with water, which was constantly pumped out. When the new pits were dug out, the concrete was poured onto plastic bags to keep the water out. When the Central Works was demolished and flats built in its place, the builders would have had the same problem. Malcolm Harris had the job of closing the works and relocating to Rothersthorpe Avenue.

Another thing that the architect would have had to take into consideration was the Sheep Path, an ancient path running from the market out of the town. As it was an ancient right of way, United Counties and the developers could not gate their site, but as this right was not generally known by the local population, United Counties did not have many problems with damage as a result.

Water from the Becket Spring, which also flowed under the works, was pumped out daily from a sump and went through a pipe into the river. However, when the pump was installed it would not work – the water was so pure that the ions were few, and would not operate the sensor. When a bucket of iron fillings was dumped into the sump, the pump began to rust and the sensor then worked.

The National Bus Company's Chief Engineer was Mr Blomfield, and Mr Robinson was the Managing Director. Other managers were Frank Gatehouse and Fred Merriman, and the Works Manager was Sid Wesley. He was followed in this job by Jock Mitchell, Gordon Heard and Malcolm Harris. When Mr Dravers was the Managing Director he was liked by the works staff, as he tried his best to get them good conditions of work and benefits – he did not always succeed, but he tried.

Fred Merriman used to live in the bungalow on the works site. He would drive the company car round the corner to work each day and one day it would not start – the battery was flat due to only travelling about 100 yards a day. Consequently, when it was sold it was not run in. Rumour had it that 'Old Jack' had died in this bungalow before the works was built and would be seen around the site, complete with his Jack Russell dog, flat cap and gabardine mac. Harvey saw him once and challenged him. He was ignored and the chap went up the stairs into the washroom. Following him, Harvey was unable to find the man.

Harvey remembers his colleagues, Mick Mullins (of the fuel injection team), who had a job keeping to time; Bill Cox, a bus driver; Fred Townsend, who worked in the Paint Shop; Colin Needle, an apprentice; Ivor Wright, a great welder; Tom Bridey, who worked on the radiators; and Sid Wesley, who was in charge when Harvey joined the company. Teddy Hater was an electrician, Neil Ingram was the chauffeur, and Richard Dunkeley, Clive Smith and Les Porter worked in the Trimming Shop, upstairs. Stanley Dean was known as 'Lightning' due to the speed of his work, Colin Gardner and John Cunningham were also in the works, and the pit crews included, in Number 1 pit, Frank Davis and apprentice John Legge, while Number 2 pit was run by Dave Miles, the floating fitter was Harry Jelly, and Bill Darby worked on the front axle dock.

Bill Law was in charge of the company car maintenance. Included in this fleet was the General Manager's car, one of which was an automatic. The GM was not used to it and went to move it but put it in the wrong gear by mistake and unfortunately pinned one of his colleagues to the wall. The colleague was rushed to hospital and walked with a limp from then onwards.

One man at the works, Brian Ward, was a local historian and seemed to know many obscure facts; he would enthral his colleagues with his knowledge.

Harvey learned to drive buses, lorries and company cars around the works site before his 21st birthday, then when he reached 21 he was taken out for a drive in Bristol KSW 838 by Maurice Hurnell, who took him round the town into Derngate, backed him up to a bay, then took him to Norman Maycock's office. Norman was pleased that he had reached the standard with one trip and offered him extra driving hours. Harvey felt he did enough hours for the company already, so was sent to Dave Parker in the Traffic Office and put on the passed driver register.

Each works area had its own operative who kept the area clean and tidy; they took a pride in their work and vied with each other to create the cleanest part of the works. One of these was Charlie March, who worked in the Body Shop.

At one time the stores were bought a second-hand Bedford TK 3½-ton lorry with a tail-lift, which was converted for its new role. The United Counties Body Shop team were known for their robust work, and in this case the lorry weighed 3½ tons when it was rebuilt and therefore could not carry any spares. It had been built by 'Pop' Mayo like a tank, with dual walls and insulation, to keep the stores warm. The lorry was therefore rebuilt using fibreglass instead of aluminium and was a lot lighter and a useful tool.

Harvey thought the Bristol SU buses, with their non-standard Albion engines, were peculiar. There were only five of them and they were used for local work. However, they had a mechanical system for working the accelerator, and when this broke it was often temporarily changed for a bit of string, which had the affect of making the bus a lot quicker (55mph instead of 45.) These vehicles were nicknamed by Bill Nicholson as the 'Fish and Chip vans'.

One icy day Harvey was road-testing Bristol FLF 637 along the Old Bedford Road, before the Barns Meadow interchange and the Nene Valley Way (A45) were even thought about. Approaching the large triangle island, at the bottom of Rushmere Road, there was a long lazy S-bend. He must have hit a patch of black ice, for the bus turned round through 360 degrees without any encouragement and continued on its way unscathed.

Other buses Harvey remembers for their problems. One was Bristol VR 777, which arrived in Derngate and dropped its Mitre box on the floor, much to the annoyance of Derrick Mould, who was duty Inspector on that date. The bus was towed backwards to the works by the recovery vehicle, with the gearbox following in the fitter's van.

Another problem bus was one of the Bristol RELH coaches, which had an engine and fuel system that was rebuilt time after time as it played up and was not as fast as the others. In the end the company gave up and replaced the engine.

When the Bristol RELL buses started to be delivered, the clutch plates only lasted for three weeks before falling apart. The Bristol works replaced the gear wheel with one with more springs (18 instead of 15), which solved the problem. One of the RELLs, 319, was a rogue and was unfortunate as it crashed three times in its career. On one occasion it was travelling over the main crossroads in Luton and was hit by a large car on its offside front wheel. The force sent it across the road and through the front of a building. The front half of the body was badly damaged and fortunately the driver had vacated his seat before it was pushed down through the floor. The bus was towed back to Northampton and after some work was done it was sent up to Southfields bus and coach restoration at Loughborough for a new body. Harvey drove it with only a Perspex front screen and two Inspector's coats on to keep off the frost. He remembered that it also paid a visit to Loughborough after one of its other bangs. The management at Northampton was using other works to help out in the 1960s and 1970s, as they had masses of their own work to do.

During one Loughborough visit Harvey saw a fitter working out in the yard doing a major engineering job under a bus, replacing the main and big end bearings. This would have been better done inside instead of on the grit and dirt. Apparently he had also done the ball joints and front wheel tapered roller bearings. Harvey was not happy, especially as the vehicle was United Counties Bristol FS 699. He went into the main office and made a confidential phone call to 'Johnny' Johnson, who was Assistant Chief Engineer at the time, and told him what was going on. From that time on Southfields did no more mechanical work. Bill Horwood and Peter Gleave were sent up to check the body work being done on United Counties vehicles.

Another RELH coach was nearly cut in half by a jack-knifed lorry and was towed, by the Kettering wrecker, to Wolverton railway works, where it was re-engined and its bodywork repaired. Harvey was steering and the works entrance was just about wide enough for the bus and wrecker. When they got to the door the wrecker was taken off and a tug was used to reverse the bus between the railway carriages. Wolverton Works had a good reputation for its standard of workmanship, but when Harvey collected the bus the replacement engine was not very good and he only just managed the 12 miles home to Northampton.

On another occasion Harvey was steering a former Birch Bros bus/coach behind the Matador as they went past the Accident & Emergency department of Northampton Hospital. An ambulance flew out and the Matador driver pulled hard over, bending the tow bar and breaking the towing eye. The Matador shot straight on at the traffic lights and the bus, following on with little braking, turned left and headed down Bedford Road hill for the works. Harvey drove into the depot front entrance and was able to stop the bus just before hitting the workshop wall. The depot team quickly chocked it up before it shot back out of the door.

Bristol MW coach 153 was coming up the M1 motorway one day with Bill Warren driving it. Bill saw a bus wheel pass him on the road and disappear up the embankment. He stopped at the next services, and when he got out of his seat the bus fell onto its nearside axle, which was minus its wheel – the bus had stayed upright due to Bill's weight. He was lucky. It took the recovery team a long time to find the wheel, which was in a neighbouring field.

Another incident involved Bristol MW coach 159, which was only two years old at the time, in 1965. It was hit by an Austin Westminster, or a Wolseley 6-110, on the A508 at the bad double bends by Kelmarsh going towards Market Harborough. The driver was Ron Farley and the car was coming towards him at speed on the wrong side of the road. Ron managed to turn hard right to avoid a head-on collision, and the car buried itself into the side of the bus instead. There was a drainage dyke on the right-hand side of the road with a line of trees beside it. The bus continued along the dyke and was stopped by the trees, which stopped it turning over. Unfortunately the lady driver and her daughter died at the incident. The car was found right under the bus, the furthest that any car had reached. The bus went back to Eastern

Coach Works for rebuilding; the damaged bodywork was taken off and the rest sheeted down. The front was exposed, with only the driver's seat, the controls and the steering left. Peter Wedgebrow was detailed to drive it over to Lowestoft. He later became the Running Shift Foreman, then went to Wellingborough Depot as Foreman.

United Counties borrowed several Eastern National Bristol FLF coaches. When they were finished with they were delivered back to Chelmsford one New Year's Eve by Peter Gleave, Colin Stockley and Bernard Deacon, with Harvey in the Bedford CF van following on behind with oil and other supplies in case they were needed.

Bristol RELH coach 293 was experimentally fitted with springs instead of air suspension by Harvey. It was then sent off for testing on a banked test track and the results were sent back to Bristol Commercial Vehicles for assessment.

Towards the end of its existence the works took on a contract to refurbish coaches, which were all painted white and sold on to a Mr Whitbread.

Harvey started his skilled career working a basic 42-hour week at £3.43 per week, and when he left he worked a basic 39 hours a week and earned £3.20 per hour. Three sets of overalls and a pair of boots were supplied every year.

Harvey became a member of the local busmen's group, known as the Midland Counties Group. They preserved old vehicles, such as Bristol L 962 and a Bedford vehicle, and would go on trips, organised by Bill Nicholson and his pals. One trip was a visit to Eastern Coach Works at Lowestoft on October ('subject to the present industrial dispute being resolved').

Sara Percy worked at the works canteen for four years in the late 1970s and early 1980s. The canteen was upstairs and Sara worked as a waitress and enjoyed the job until she left due to a misunderstanding. This was where she met and from where she married Harvey. Harvey and Sara took part in Social Club activities, including Harvey playing skittles with Ray Neil. Some social functions were organised by the wives of Len Flattery and Graham Roberts, as they worked at the hospital next door, which had a suite for this use.

Following his United Counties career Harvey worked for many other companies, including Luton & District buses for six months, Northampton Transport (First Group), Country Lion buses, Soul's coaches, Stagecoach buses, Blackwood Hodge (earth-moving vehicle manufacturers) and an engine-building company, and now works as a part-time security guard all round the county.

3
Rothersthorpe Avenue

These works replaced the Bedford Road Works when they closed in 1990, due to the company becoming smaller after deregulation in 1987 and the subsequent purchase of United Counties by Stagecoach Holdings. The works and Head Office buildings were too large for the staff required by the new owners.

The site was originally the Rothersthorpe Road Garage, which was defunct. AWD Northampton trucks were using the part of the site when it was purchased, and it was developed over the following 20 years; at the time of writing it is still in use as a works and head office only, most of the buses being garaged at Greyfriars Bus Station.

Right: **Rothersthorpe Avenue staff and engineers raising money for the 'Pink Day' charity in November 2007.** *Stagecoach East collection*

Below: **The Rothersthorpe Avenue Works site in Northampton.** *Roger Warwick collection*

Tony Cox

Tony has been a bus boy and man all his life – apparently one of his first words was 'bus'. Coming from Maidstone in Kent, his first job after getting a degree in Economics was three months driving, in 1976. He cycled the 3 miles there and back daily. When the manager asked why he should train him up for three months, Tony's reply was that the company was desperate for drivers and he could help. He still holds a licence for driving, and has a driving job to go back to when he wants it. He is also active in the bus preservation world, having shares in three vehicles back in Kent. His driving licence is useful for this, too, as he learned to drive on 'crash gearbox' vehicles.

On leaving college, Tony was awarded a place on the two-year NBC training programme. He was allocated to Trent for a start, followed by 12 months at the Stroud Depot of Bristol Omnibus, working with Tony Collins. Next was Ribble, with a Depot Manager's jobs at Lancaster, Morecambe and Garstang, followed by Area Manager North, including the above and Kendal, Penrith and Carlisle. Ian Chapman was the General Manager at that time.

Stagecoach bought Ribble soon after this and Brian Souter offered Tony a position at United Counties, so in 1987 Tony came to Northampton for the first time. At the time of his arrival, United Counties was starting to restructure financially and business-wise. Bedford was the biggest depot and the one needing most financial help. Brian had made a start and Tony was brought in to help turn the company into a profitable unit, which Tony was able to do as part of a team that included Ben Colson, Barry Warner and Brian Souter himself.

After three years of effort, Tony made a sideways move to First Bus, as Regional Manager for Essex, based at Chelmsford. This post then included depots at Northampton (formerly Northampton Corporation Transport), Leicester (formerly Leicester City Corporation) and Wyvern Buses (formerly Midland Red West).

In 1994 Tony returned to Stagecoach as Regional Manager Kent, South and East (including the former United Counties), which is his present post. However, from September 2007 Tony has been acting General Manager at Stagecoach East. This is very useful as he and his family have lived in the area since joining Stagecoach United Counties in the 1980s. His present job is much the same as before, but with only small problems needing to be sorted this time.

Managing Director Tony Cox with Nick Shipton and Lenny Stolarski. *Brian Hadden and Kettering team collection*

For the future, Tony is looking to expand the business, with more housing likely in the area and more passengers coming back to buses from cars, due to rapid cost rises.

Sandra Fawcett, née Cripps

Sandra comes from a United Counties bus family. Both her grandfather Frank Cripps (1953-68) and father Thomas Cripps (1960-66) worked in Northampton, one a conductor and the other an apprentice at the works. One story Sandra remembers concerns her father and a friend, who went on a coach tour to London. Missing the coach back, they wondered how to get home. Finding a bus at Victoria with a back window missing, they drove it back to Northampton, left it at the back of the works and went home. However, they had to thaw out as the bus was freezing cold. Sandra imagines that there were scratched heads at the works as to how this bus had arrived.

Sandra started working for Stagecoach United Counties in 1995, where she was part of the Accounts team until it was disbanded in 1999. From that time she remembers her colleagues Richard Oakley, Coleen Coates, Alison Donnelly, Ian McIlwaine, Karen Hines, Wendy Flinders, Amanda Hopper and Wendy Cox. When all the others left, Sandra was on her own and had to tidy up the office and take up all the work left to do.

Sandra remembers Roger Warwick at Rothersthorpe Avenue before he retired, Phillip Norwell, Howard Butler, Steve Chambers, Terry Gordon, Colin Stockley and Mr and Mrs Westley.

Sandra has done many jobs during her 12 years with the company. She is now the company's first port of call, on the telephone and in person, in reception. She also looks after the retired staff passes and deals with accidents. At the time of writing she is also intending to learn to drive a bus.

The accounts team at Rothersthorpe Avenue on the day they disbanded. *Sandra Cripps collection*

Mike Summers and the late Tom Poulter

Mike Summers works at Northampton for Stagecoach East, where he and Tom Poulter worked together as instructors and became good friends until the latter's death. Mike met Tom as a trainee driver in September 1995, as Tom was his instructor. He also knew Roger Warwick and Steve Loveridge well, both of whom were at Tom's funeral in April 2008. Mike supplied the following memories.

✳

Last year Stagecoach made my position as instructor redundant, and the classroom we used was cleared of pictures, many of which were old pictures of the training fleet and the old depot in Bedford Road. An NVQ

officer now works in this office and the last time I saw it there was nothing from the school days on display.

Tom would have loved to have been able to contribute to this work and was a well-loved character. He told me many stories about 'the old days' and I loved to kid with him because he was like Uncle Albert in TV's *Only Fools and Horses*. When Tom used to say 'In the old days…' we would all tell him to shut up, but we loved to hear his tales, although they were about things that may not be suitable for this book.

Willie Lawson lost his position at the same time as me and now runs his own bus on school contracts. Fortunately, Stagecoach kept me on in the role of Monitor/Relief Instructor. Bob Beeston from Kettering Depot also left and is operating his own bus, undertaking training for teachers and other things. I worked from Northampton Depot regarding training,

The Stagecoach East training team: (l-r) Bob Beeston (Kettering), Mike Summers (Northampton), Fred Hooton (Kettering), John Appleton (Examiner), William Lawson (Corby), Tom Poulter (Northampton), Colin Albone (Bedford), and Mick Campbell (Kettering). Tom's training bus was 1008, on the left of the photograph. *Jackie Bazeley collection*

but like Tom, Brian, Willie, Bob and Fred Hooton we covered all depots. Some years back Willie and I were made up to salaried pay and I came under Head Office. However, I still spent most of my time at Northampton.

I held an ADI (Approved Driving Instructor) badge and also worked as a driving examiner for the Department of Transport Driving Standards Agency (DSA) for some years before joining Stagecoach. I started in September 1995, which is how I met Tom.

After a short time I was made driver/mentor, then after about three years I joined the training school under John Appleton working alongside Tom and the others. Tom and I became good friends, and I am still in contact with some of his family.

Tom was a wonderful guy, robust and with a zest for life like no other person I knew. He changed my life, enriched it, and I miss him terribly. Strangely, on 25 June last year my father died and I took Tom to buy a new car on the same day just to find a distraction. He was as fit as always, yet little did I know that I would lose him too within ten months.

Tom was a creature of habit. When I came to work in the morning he would be in the same seat with his bag on the desk in the same place with an orange cut into pieces on silver foil. He would also be reading – he loved westerns and pirate stories. He kept every book he ever bought and would sometimes read them again. However, he rarely got any peace once I arrived, as I loved talking with him about fishing and Koi-keeping, two of Tom's favourite hobbies. By this time he was semi-retired and worked from 9.00am until 2.00pm, and when he went home he was one of those people who left work at work. He had a life outside Stagecoach, which he loved.

Tom was loved by all because he trained most of the drivers at the depot. 'I'm just a genie granting wishes to those less fortunate than me,' he used to say, meaning getting drivers their licences. Sometimes new drivers would come back to him and say that they hated the job, and Tom would remind them that he had granted their wish at the time and was not responsible for the outcome. He had a dry sense of humour.

Tom and I were like two naughty schoolchildren; he was in the fifth year and I was a first-year newbie. He talked me into all sorts of things and we laughed about our capers. One day he talked me into going with him in the training bus to buy some bits for his garden. 'It will be OK,' he said, but we were seen carrying two rain butts and several litres of fencing paint across the car park. On another occasion we went to buy fishing tackle for me, and Tom said we would go to Wellingborough, where we would not be seen. We parked the training bus in Church Street Bus Station, when it was quiet, but on our return found that the service buses had not been

able to get into their bays, because the training bus was blocking the entire street. We effectively closed central Wellingborough.

Drivers would sometimes say to Tom that they saw the training bus outside fishing shops all over Northamptonshire and Tom would say, 'That will be Mike. I'll have a word with him.' Of course, the drivers knew the truth because Tom took them all to fishing shops when he trained them. 'No point in having all this power if you don't abuse it,' he would sometimes say. Tom was serious about his training, though, and he did not suffer fools gladly. He had a great pass rate and was good at what he did.

The first time I met Tom was on my assessment day, a baking hot day in August. I was in a three-piece suit sitting in the canteen drinking a cold can of soft drink and looking out at the buses coming and going. Suddenly a voice broke the silence. 'It's no good you looking at those modern things,' it said. 'What you've got to drive is much more difficult.' I was already nervous, and this made me feel really great as you can imagine. When I saw the bus I tried to lighten the moment by saying, 'Do we have to stoke the boilers before we can move it?' Tom's reply was, 'Don't worry about that because if you want this job you've got to get me around the course. Let's see if you're still laughing when you get back.'

Like all the old hands, Tom was passionate about buses, especially old buses. This is the only thing I never had in common with Tom: to me they are just machines. Still, I made the course and the rest, as they say, is history.

Tom hated gadgets, any gadget. He laughed at me with my mobile phone, my PDA and my talk about computers. He used to listen to my discussions about PC problems and would say, 'When you get home tonight, lock the door where you keep that PC, throw away the key and go out and get some fresh air.' As much has Tom influenced me over the years, I also started to influence him. He bought a mobile phone, although he rarely switched it on, and when he did he would go out and leave it on the kitchen table. I used to moan at him that his kids could not get hold of him. 'Listen,' he'd say, 'I've managed 60-plus years without one.' At 72 years old Tom bought his first PC and, although I spent many an hour fixing it, it was not long before he was burning his own music and buying on Ebay.

I hope I've given you an insight into Tom, and I hope that my love for this man shows through. In Tom's day, work was simple and somehow more efficient. Today, the bus industry is a different world. The buses are easier to drive, but the demands of driving and training are much harder. Tom would often quote 'KISS: Keep It Simple Stupid'. What a shame that we've lost sight of that.

Keith Dyball

Keith is a new recruit to Stagecoach East, having joined in December 2006 as Engineering Director. Keith's career has always been in road transport. He started with the British Army as an apprentice technician. When he came out at the age of 30 after 12 years, he worked as Central Works Manager for Geest Bananas.

After a while he acquired a post as Fleet Engineer and moved into the bus industry with Midland Fox at Leicester a short while after privatisation. This company had a very unprofitable maintenance operation, with some vehicles off the road for a week or more awaiting parts. He upped the spares to 20% from 6% to alleviate this.

Keith was offered the carrot of a manager's job for a new depot at Thurmaston, shared with a recovery company, and his job was taken over by another person. When the new depot was nearly finished the owners of Midland Fox were taken to court over financial irregularities and the depot went, together with Keith's job.

Blackburn needed an Engineering Manager, and was then taken over by Burnley & Pendle, a Stagecoach company. Brian Souter transferred Keith to Engineering Manager at East Kent and thence to Stagecoach East.

He has Engineering Managers at Bedford (Wayne Bartrum), Northampton (Tony Gates) and Garry Line (Kettering). All three are younger recruits and are being groomed and trained for their next career move as Engineering Directors with Stagecoach. Part of their training is a six-month residential HNC course (in management) in Bristol. Keith also has apprentices at Kettering (three) and Northampton (two), who are being trained to NVQ111 standard. Keith believes that all work should be done in-house if at all possible to make work more economic.

Michelle Hargreaves

Michelle has been in the bus industry for most of her career. She started 20 years ago with Ribble buses at Blackburn as a cash clerk and was the only woman at the depot. She then moved into the traffic team and became a driver. Later in her career she became Operations Manager at Blackburn and Operations Manager at Chorley, then at her largest depot at Lancaster. In 2000 she became the Traffic Manager at Stagecoach East and a Director of the company in November 2000.

Michelle's first job was as a store detective at the Co-op, and the skills acquired in this post have been good for her bus career. She was beaten up one year and this persuaded her to get a new job. Her new career came out of the Job Centre and she does not

Michelle Hargreaves and Brian Laywood on his retirement from Kettering. *Brian Hadden and Kettering team collection*

regret the move.

Michelle tries to get to know all her staff, attending induction days to greet them and meeting them on her rounds. All staff know who she is and what she does.

Michelle manages three Operations Managers – Brian Hadden, Zoe Paget and Mark Butler – and reports to the Managing Director and to Brian Souter, whom she sees about three times a year. Michelle also reports to the UK Bus Managing Director, Les Warneford. She is concerned that only four Operations Director posts are filled by women, and the next step for her is to be a General Manager.

In late 2008 Michelle was appointed Managing Director for Stagecoach in Devon.

Arthur Michell

Arthur did not work for United Counties but was a teacher at Roade School, and part of his responsibilities was the school minibus.

Arthur remembers taking the minibus into Rothersthorpe Avenue one morning and talking to Mr W. H. Bailey, the MOT assessor. Arthur felt very proud that Mr Bailey's last MOT was for the minibus.

When he retired, Arthur owned a depository for 70 vehicles (including some former United Counties vehicles) and now owns another depository for 32 vehicles (some of which are also former United Counties vehicles).

Arthur remembers more of the Northampton Corporation vehicles than United Counties and Stagecoach, and organises vintage Northampton vehicles for the annual Heritage weekend in September at Northampton. Arthur also remembers Howard Butler, who worked for United Counties.

4
Derngate Bus Station
and Bedford Road Depot

Built between 1934 and 1937, Derngate was described as the one of the few covered bus and coach stations in the country and was probably the finest of its type. It replaced many temporary bus stations around the town.

The building served United Counties well until 1976, when Northampton's Development Corporation built the new Greyfriars Bus Station to serve most Northampton Transport and United Counties services. Derngate survived until 1980 when it was demolished and replaced by the present-day Derngate entertainment complex.

Bedford Road Garage was opened in 1923 as a basic unit and occupied the site of the later main works buildings. To get to it the buses had to negotiate a narrow lane. A replacement garage was built in 1936 nearer to the Bedford Road and had much improved facilities. The deopt closed at the same time as the site was sold in 1990. However, most of the vehicles were actually garaged in Greyfriars Bus Station by that time.

A view of Derngate Bus Station, showing the exit door and layover area on the right. The service bays were numbered 1-14 from right to left, and there was a bus wash in the roof. Behind the photographer are the coach bays, fuel bays and the bus entrance. *Roger Warwick collection*

George Lucas

George Lucas's daughter Joan Jones contributes this account of her father's career.

My father joined the Wellingborough Bus Company in 1919, after serving in the First World War; as many lads did, he exaggerated his age and signed on for the Army at 15.

When George married my mother they went to live in Ecton and he became a conductor in Northampton, working for Grose's, which later became part of United Counties. When I was four years old we moved to the St James area of Northampton.

I have many memories of being taken by my Dad to Houghton Road Garage, which at that time was the only United Counties depot in Northampton, before Derngate Bus Station was built.

The staff did not have a canteen and used two places in Northampton, Nappins in Horseshoe Street and the café in the Mayorhold. Staff were allowed to take in their own food if they wished to. When my father was on a route through St James, my mother would take out his dinner as he passed.

The men decided to have a canteen of their own, and they all donated a small sum to start it off. It was run by former driver George Blunt, who had been involved in a bad accident in a double-decker bus near the Plough Hotel in Northampton, and was unable to drive again as a result. The canteen proved to be a great asset, as the men could buy their food at low prices, as they did not intend to make a profit. When Derngate Bus Station opened it was a wonderful thing and a grand place at that time.

Although the company continued to grow there was always a great rapport among the men. In those days the driver and the conductor used to work together all the time. Dad had three drivers: Les Bree was his regular driver, while Horace Holmes and Alf Bishop also drove for him. Les Bree was a bit of a comic, and when they took a bus on a new route the villagers used to line the main street to welcome them. Les would wear a yellow duster as a cravat and bow from side to side to the villagers.

Before the Second World War the staff of drivers and conductors went on strike to have a paid holiday. I was very worried, as my Mum said that if my father did not go back to work soon we only had a Christmas pudding in the larder, although I think she was exaggerating a bit.

In early 1939 my Dad became an Inspector after having been a driver for some years. When the war came in September of that year the company was very busy at all the depots. The Ministry of Defence could commandeer buses and crews at short notice, using them to take the forces from place to place.

There was quite a funny incident involving a young man in Yardley Hastings. Being slightly mentally disabled, he lived with his Mum and Dad and was unable to work. As a lad he had been given a conductor's whistle. He stood on one of the village bus stops and it became usual that the bus did not leave the stop until Freddy blew his whistle. However, when war broke out whistles were banned. My father was sent to visit Freddy's parents to see what could be done. Freddy had rotten front teeth, which he did not realise, so his mother told him that blowing the whistle would rot his teeth. Freddy still stood at the bus stop for many years and saw off the buses, but did not blow his whistle again.

I think it was 1942 when a Wellington bomber crash-landed in front of All Saints Church in Northampton. My Dad was on the early shift, in Derngate, at 5.30am. I was poorly, so that morning Dad brought me a drink and said he had to go as he was late already. Dad was never late, so that was terrible for him. As he went along the hall we heard a thud, but did not know what it was. When Dad got to the bottom of Gold Street the wings of the plane were down in the street and he had to go round by way of the Cattle Market and along Albion Place, on the other side of Derngate. As he arrived at work, a busman came out and said that he was about to report Dad as missing under the wreckage, and thank goodness he was all right! George replied that he might have been under it if Joan had not felt ill. He told me later that I had saved his life.

Many of the young busmen were called up into the forces during the war. In their place were the 'clippies', who proved to be very hard-working and were some lovely ladies. One of them came to lodge with us. Her name was Mildred Major, from Plymouth. After the war Mum and Dad used to visit Mildred and her family, and they came to Northampton.

In 1960 my father suffered two major heart attacks and had to finish as an Inspector. He was then employed in the offices at Derngate, over the Booking Office, until he retired in 1964. His favourite story was that he worked in this office with the future entertainer Des O'Connor.

My father died in 1977 at the age of 77, and I know that his 45 years with United Counties were very happy ones.

Harry ('Joe') Beckett

Angela Seelig, Joe's granddaughter, recalls that Joe started working for United Counties in 1931. He started off driving Leyland Lion buses, then after a while graduated to driving the Bristol LL coaches with

Above: Joe Beckett with a Tilling Stevens bus owned by Clarke Brothers of Weedon. That company was taken over by United Counties on 29 December 1930, but this was never a United Counties bus. *Angela Seelig collection*

Below: The coach contingent, in a photograph thought to have been taken in the 1940s. The front row includes Peter Patchesa (second from left) and Joe Beckett (fourth from left). *Angela Seelig collection*

Above: Joe Beckett in his back garden in Northampton. He is in his United Counties uniform. *Angela Seelig collection*

LORRY CRASHES INTO BUS

OUT OF CONTROL ON "TRAGIC" NORTHANTS ROAD

MAN SERIOUSLY HURT

HELPLESS in the cabin of his lorry which skidded and got out of control on the ice-covered road near Chapel Brampton early to-day, Harold Argyle (26), of Ratby, Leicestershire, was seriously injured, and had to be taken to the Northampton General Hospital.

The lorry crashed head-on into a United Counties double-decker bus. It narrowly missed a cottage, standing by the bridge over the Nene, in which live Mr. and Mrs. Jeyes and their four young children.

Argyle is a married man with one child.

The lorry, owned by W. D. Warner and Son, of Markfield, Leicester, was laden with paving stones and was travelling to Northampton from the direction of Leicester. The bus, driven by Mr. W. H. Beckett, of Northampton, had just passed the Boughton railway crossing and had reached the bridge over the Nene. The driver saw that an accident was inevitable and he pulled up. The only other person in the bus was Mr. P. Patchesa, the conductor.

The lorry, if it had not been for the bus, would have crashed through the wall and into the Nene.

WOMAN HELPS

The first person on the scene of the accident was Mrs. Jeyes. Her husband, a farm worker on Karl Spencer's estate, recently returned from six weeks in hospital with a poisoned hand, and was unable to help, but his wife volunteered assistance, and she went with the ambulance to the hospital.

A few seconds after the accident an old friend of Argyle, Donald Timpson, of Glenfield, Leicestershire, drove by with his lorry. He has known Argyle for many years. He pulled up.

Mrs. Jeyes told a Chronicle and Echo reporter that her family was in bed when the accident happened.

"I heard a crash and cries of 'Help, help,' and moans. I got up and the children screamed. My husband told me not to go out, but I could not stop in. The conductor rushed to the phone for the ambulance and I went with him and the man to the hospital. I only brought my husband back from there on Sunday. This is a tragic road and my children want us to move.

"'Don't stop here any longer, mummy,' they said after the accident. We have only been here two years and this is the fourth accident we have had."

NEARLY ANOTHER ACCIDENT

Caption: SMASH.—The lorry which skidded at Chapel Brampton and crashed with a United Counties bus. The lorry just missed the cottage.

Above: In December 1935 Joe and his conductor Peter Patchesa were in a United Counties double-decker bus at Boughton when this lorry hit them. The bus was stationary and the lorry driver had skidded on ice. *Angela Seelig collection*

Below: Joe was driving this Bristol LL6B, FRP 839, in June 1951 when it caught on fire near Victoria Coach Station, London. Here the flames are being put out by the firemen. The coach was rebuilt and sold on to Thames Valley Buses in 1958. *Angela Seelig collection*

Above: Brand-new OBD 902 is seen during a trip round the depots to show it off, probably in 1957. Northampton driver Len Bull is at the helm with Joe Beckett at the window. *Angela Seelig collection*

24 walked out

Twenty-four people had an uneventful 120-mile journey from Nottingham to London yesterday. They neared Victoria, S.W., then . . . the coach burst into flames. Passengers got out, unhurt, and dragged their luggage clear—and the fire brigade tackled the blaze, ABOVE.

Lutman, Bob Coote, Percy Greaves, Nora Brown, Mrs Allen, Phyllis Perkins, Eileen Stevens, Shirley Watt with a youthful Roger Warwick on the back seat. *Angela Seelig collection*

Below and opposite middle & bottom: **Some of the busmen's coach trips. In the first photograph Joe is fourth from the left, then Harold Clipston, Edwin Horner fourth from the right, and Herbert Leathersich second from right. In the second Joe is under open cab window, and in the third he on the extreme left, in the dark suit, Harold Clipston is third from the left, and Cyril Green fourth from the right.** *All Angela Seelig collection*

Above: **Len Gentle, Joe Beckett and Len Bull converse inside Aylesbury Depot during the trip.** *Angela Seelig collection*

Above right: **A publicity shot of brand-new 250 FRP, driven by Joe Beckett, taken at Collingtree on the A508. Others on the bus include Peter**

Above: **Joe Beckett (second from right) receives a safe driving award from Norman Maycock (extreme left). Others present are, from the left, Len Bull, Jack Hartley, Frank Johnson, Harold Clipston, Ken Wellman, Tommy Read, Albert ('Peggy') Stevens, Mick Kelly, Fred Archer, Maurice Hurnell, John Coles and Doug Freeman.** *Northampton Chronicle & Echo, Angela Seelig collection*

Joe later became a driving instructor and eventually the Chief Driving Instructor. *Angela Seelig collection*

When Joe officially retired in 1973 he was presented with a gift by Brian Horner (Traffic Manager) and George Sell, on behalf of his colleagues. *NBC News, Angela Seelig collection*

John Birks presided at another presentation. *Angela Seelig collection*

Right: **Back row (l-r): Sid Wesley, Frank Johnson, Albert Houghton, Sam Cockerill, Fred Merriman, Albert Stevens (nicknamed 'Peggy' after his old bus), Jack Hartley, Norman Maycock and Fred Doughty. Front row (l-r): Frank Woska, Jack Garlic, Fred Archer, Joe Beckett and Reg Mitchell.** *Angela Seelig collection*

other coach drivers. Later coaches were Bristol LSs and Bristol RELHs. His claim to fame was driving 250 FRP on its first trip down the M1 motorway on service MX1. United Counties was very proud of its new bus and wanted to show it off. These new buses had to have microphones fitted to the engine compartment, so that the driver could hear the engine noise, the reason being that there had been problems with burned-out clutches.

Joe, on the extreme right, also received a 40-year long service award from United Counties. Others pictured include Jim Burley, W. Gravestock and Les Bidewell. *Angela Seelig collection*

In 1974 Joe (back row, second from left) attended a dinner at the Angel Hotel in Northampton. Others present include R. Pates, G. Jacob, V. Webb, H. Warnes, Maurice Jewitt, Len Gentle, Harold Clipston, Jack Hartley, P. Russell, H. Houghton and E. Claridge. The picture was taken at Bedford Road. *NBC News*

Finally Angela remembers that one of the conductresses was called Emily Burns. Joe's post was taken over by John Appleton and Norman Redhead jointly.

Jim Billingham

Jim was taught to drive a car by Joe Beckett, who lived at 19 Penrhyn Road, Far Cotton, and used to cycle to Derngate to work. When he worked for Clarks, Joe used to have a bus stop on Horseshoe Road, Daventry. Jim's father built Yardley Hastings outstation, and Michael Billingham was a manager at United Counties.

Vicky Osbourne, née Roff

Vicky was a clerk in the office at Derngate Booking Office, working there from 1940 to 1943, starting at the age of 19. She dealt with the timetable enquiries for Associated Motorways.

During the week there were three booking clerks on duty, and the hours were 8.30am to 5.30pm. Vicky had an early lunch on Fridays (usually in the Derngate coffee shop). She remembers that another of her jobs was to give out the wages to the staff, up to 500 a week. Her colleagues included Norah Court and Miss Abbott.

As Vicky worked at Derngate during the war she remembers that Sunday nights were very busy, with servicemen returning to their units. They would mainly be booked on the 5.45pm and 6.15pm coaches to Nottingham. As Vicky was usually on her own, she worked very hard. Numbers were given to the Duty Inspector, who organised coaches. Vicky also remembers that many people were evacuated to Northampton, and that many of them worked as conductresses.

Eileen Davis

Mrs Davis was Miss Paddock when she worked for United Counties. She had been bombed out of the East End of London and came to be near family friends in Northampton. She stayed in lodgings and applied for a conductress's job at Derngate Bus Station, working for the company for five years before returning to London. However, her fiancé was a fitter for United Counties, and after a year they were married and returned to live in Moulton.

Mrs Davis remembers that she worked on two shifts, 6.00am-2.00pm and 2.00pm-10.00pm. The longest route she worked on was the trip to Aylesbury, with a total job time of 5 hours. She liked the market at Aylesbury, and the café. However, this job only came her way once a year. The other long-haul journey was to Corby, which lasted 3 hours.

At night during the war the driver had difficulty driving with filtered headlamps, while back in the bus the conductress had a lamp in a tin on a wire, which she pulled along the upper deck to see what she was doing.

In the early war days, buses were only allowed eight people standing, but later, as more people used the buses, this was extended to 12 standing, although that number caused problems as the conductress had a squash to get through to get the fares.

At 5.00pm on workdays Derngate Bus Station was packed with people waiting to get home. Some conductresses packed the bus with as many as possible to get them all home.

As there were no road signs during the war, Mrs Davis never new where she was and asked the passengers getting on where they came from. As a result she became very friendly with some of them and they were pleased to see her on their bus after that.

One of the last buses to leave Derngate, at about 10.00pm, was the soldiers' bus for Overstone Park, which was apparently used extensively during the war as a camp.

Some wartime ticket prices were Kettering, 2s 3d return or 1s 3d single; Moulton, 7d return or 4d single; and Duston 5d return or 3d single.

Mrs Davis had a different driver every week; some were good and others rattled her nearly off the back! She remembers the canteen at Derngate being very good, which was useful when on fire-watching duty at night. Fire-watching paid 5 shillings a night, but most of the time the watchers played cards and drank tea in the canteen.

Ruth Eyres

These reminiscences from the Northampton Chronicle & Echo archives date from October 1978.

In 1941-45 I was a conductor and driver on United Counties buses. There were six of us doing this dual job, and my memories of conducting and driving in the blackout are still vivid. We only had one small light on each deck, covered by a deep cocoa-tin-shaped cover, which we pulled along with a piece of cord as we took the fares. I remember watching the passengers stepping out of the very dimly lit bus into the pitch-black country villages, to struggle home with tiny torches.

On busy days we took our turn on driving double-deckers out to Raunds, Daventry, Welford, Market Harborough and Aylesbury. All buses had very small headlights and, though private cars were few and far between, we often met long convoys of Army lorries.

But I remember the cheerfulness of the passengers too, who, in spite of the long hours at work and meagre rations, would joke and laugh with us. I also remember seeing the excitement of the men in the forces when home on leave and boarding the bus back to their wives and sweethearts for a few short days, often seeing them again on their return, bidding tearful goodbyes at the bus stop.

On Wednesdays at Stowe IX Churches, one passenger who boarded the bus to go to the cattle market at Northampton used to present the conductor with a fresh egg. This was a luxury and was carefully stored in our ticket box.

Thomas Higgs

Mr Higgs's son recalls that his father started with Northampton Corporation as a conductor in the 1940s, before being transferred to United Counties at Northampton in 1951. At that Mr Higgs's son travelled with his father at weekends to such places as Bedford and Oxford. Unfortunately father and son didn't get on – the former's temperament perhaps due to having being a prisoner of war three times during the conflict – and as a result his son left and moved to Yorkshire to be with his sister.

Bob Lloyd

Bob Lloyd joined United Counties in 1952, became a driver and graduated to driving motorway coaches in 1956. In 1967 Bob became an Inspector at Derngate Bus Station and finally left the area in the 1970s to work for Crosville in North Wales. Bob recalls that he was not a 'Hitler' and hopefully was firm but fair. The Inspectors used to take it in turns to go out on the road; they had the use of a company vehicle, at that time a Ford, and a uniformed lady driver.

One of Bob's double-decker memories relates to a party of nuns. Bob took a Lodekka to Pitsford and was taking the nuns to Northampton's Castle station. The journey was uneventful until Bob swung into the station to drop them off, when he heard a thunderous sound and saw poles flying past his window. The nuns hurried off the bus and Bob moved out of the way. The noise had been the station sign, which came tumbling down and left a big dent in the roof of the bus. Fortunately no one was hurt, but Bob had to own up to the British Railways authorities for his accident.

However, this was not so traumatic, as when he sheepishly took the bus to the works at Houghton Road and saw the Foreman, Jock Mitchell, Jock checked his records and said, 'Don't worry, someone else dented the bus.' Bob thus got away only lightly with that mishap.

Talking about mishaps, Bob remembers one occasion when Inspector Sam Cockerill at Derngate Bus Station saw what he presumed to be a driven Leyland bus backing into a bay, without the help of the conductor. He rushed over

Coach drivers Bob Lloyd and Jim Bowden enjoy a pint after their working day. Jim went on to drive the Bedford OB converted stores lorry/bus. *Bob Lloyd collection*

and guided the bus back, but the driver ignored his guidance and the bus crashed through the barrier and narrowly missed the outside wall of the bus station. Sam went to remonstrate with the driver and to his horror found no one there – the bus had moved on its own.

Some drivers and conductors did not need any supervision, but a few might be 'on the fiddle' and the Inspectors, including Sam and Wally Cockerill, had to catch them being fraudulent. One day Mr Maycock, the Superintendent at Derngate Bus Station, asked Bob to go and catch a conductor who was fiddling the company. He made his way to the Queen Eleanor monument and awaited the bus. When it arrived he checked all the tickets and talked to the passengers. Apparently the conductor was picking up old tickets from the floor, reselling them and pocketing the money. The conductor was sacked.

Disputes happened from time to time at Derngate Bus Station. One arose because a conductor had been drinking on duty. The Swan Hotel (now The Mailcoach) was the favoured pub for most staff at Derngate. One day a driver who was on a spare turn and was not needed went over to the pub to wait. He had been a thorn in the side of the Inspectors and they wanted rid of him, so one of them went over to the Swan and bought him a drink. When he went back to sign off he was called into the office and sacked. The driver was so incensed that he went down and told the other staff what had occurred. All the driving and conducting staff went on strike, a bus was used to block the exit, and no bus left for 3 hours, after which he was reinstated and the strike finished.

United Counties operated scheduled coach runs to London, Nottingham, Cambridge and Cheltenham as part of the Associated Motorways group of services, and in the summer these services were extended to all parts of the country. They used vehicles and drivers from all the companies in the group.

Bob remembers his first coach trip. The Inspectors were short of a driver and Bob was asked to help. He was given a 33-seater L Type Bristol coach, in Royal Blue colours. The luggage rack was on the roof and accessed by a ladder up the back. Bob had to load the rack by himself, then put a canvas cover over the luggage, which he securely fixed. The trip itself was uneventful and Bob was regularly used as a coach driver thereafter.

In the 1950s coaches were restricted to 30mph on most roads. This caused problems if they were running late. Most London services used the A5 south of Northampton and this was good for speedy runs between towns.

Coach drivers had to stay away on some turns, as it took 3hr 20min from London to Northampton, and 2hr 30min from Northampton to Nottingham. With a stop-over turn, the driver left Victoria Coach Station in London at 8.30am; between turns the coaches were parked at Samuelsons coach garage, across the road from Victoria. The driver had a 2-hour break in Northampton before carrying on for Nottingham at 2.00pm. Meanwhile his morning coach had gone on at 12.00 noon to Nottingham with another driver. At Nottingham Bob would have a break, then drive back to Northampton before signing off. This was a 14- or 15-hour day.

One day Bob was driving a duplicate coach to the main service coach – it was a 37-seater and a good drive. The service coach was driven by Reg Welford, and he left on time. Bob was instructed to wait for 15 hired vehicles to come in before he left. By the time all were ready to go, Bob had four seats spare and was 13//4 hours late leaving. To make up time he put his foot down and the Smith's milometer reached its 50mph limit. Bob picked up at Golders Green, then headed for home. At Markyate he was stopped by a car driver, who had a broken windscreen – he alleged that a bottle had been thrown out of the coach window and smashed the glass. No one would own up, so Bob left the driver with his details and rushed off. At Dunstable he made a quick toilet stop for the passengers, then headed up the A5. He had just been passed by a sports car when he noticed a tall aerial in his mirror and heard a bell ringing. He was pulled over by a police car, having apparently been speeding at 62mph. He was let off with a caution when he explained that he was late and trying to make up time.

This was not the only time that Bob was pulled up. Once he was stopped for allegedly speeding at 82mph. Again he was let off with a caution. However, this was while working for Crosville with an Olympian on the Coastliner service to Chester from Llandudno. The company asked the drivers to cut the time allowed from 2hr 50min to 2hr 32min, which resulted in the alleged speeding to keep to time.

One day Bob was hired out to Associated Motorways and asked to take an overnight bag. Thinking that he would be back next day, he said he would. He drove to Leicester to meet the Black & White coach and followed it to Cheltenham, expecting to sleep over and go home on the same run. Unfortunately, Associated Motorways was so short of drivers that, once they had one, they tried to keep him. On arrival at Cheltenham, Bob was immediately sent to Tenby and thus started a nine-day working week. On the ninth day Bob was fed up when he arrived at Cheltenham. Fortunately, the Inspector was missing, the Cambridge coach was already on Bay 2, Bob knew the driver and they shared out the passengers, leaving before the Inspector could catch them. Bob did not volunteer again for that job.

On another occasion Bob came back off a London trip and was asked to take out a trip to Wicksteed Park in Kettering. His conductor was Percy and he was given a former Eastern National Bristol KSW with a silver radiator. All went well until the Northampton

Road bridge in Kettering; coaches and single-deckers could pass under, but all others had to go up to the other bridge on Rothwell Road. Being so used to coaches, Bob did not think and went through the bridge. Fortunately, he went through the centre and did not take the roof off, but it must have been a near thing as the conductor was going ballistic on the bell to get him to stop.

David Lloyd

David Lloyd worked as a conductor for United Counties from the age of 18 to 21 in the 1960s. It was a good time to work on the buses, with all the girls in their miniskirts! David's father and two of his three brothers also worked for United Counties. Hs father, Bob, was a driver and Inspector, one brother was a fitter and the other a driver; the third brother worked as a coach driver for Wesley Tours. David worked part-time at first because he was under-age for a full-time conductor's post. He used to work evenings and weekends when he became full-time.

David remembers many occurrences, of which the following are just a few. With Tommy Kehoe as his driver, he was sent to Aylesbury on the 346 route. They made good time and arrived at Aylesbury on time. As they had a good few minutes for the turn-round, Tommy went off to a betting shop. He was a long time, so David went to find him. The horse that Tommy was going to back was not running, so David suggested one called Kelly's Image. The bet was placed and the crew returned to their bus and loaded the passengers, pushchairs and parcels. Tommy disappeared again. David went back to the betting shop to find Tommy collecting his winnings, and all was happy.

The crew then set off back to Northampton and all was well until the Whitchurch Garage stop. Tommy could not get the bus to go – the brakes were stuck on. David went into the garage and rang Aylesbury for a replacement bus. 'We have not got any,' said the supervisor. 'You will have to get it going yourself.'

David then obtained a hammer from the garage mechanic, and started bashing the brakes to free them off, but it did not work. Then the roving Inspector arrived in his van. 'Why have you not rung for a replacement?' The situation was explained, so the Inspector made a rude call to Aylesbury. 'I want a bus here in 10 minutes!' he ordered. A bus duly arrived shortly afterwards. However, Aylesbury had sent the only vehicle that moved, the tree-lopper. It was filthy dirty and had an open roof. Fortunately, all the passengers fitted on the lower deck, so no one got too cold or wet. The engine was in need of attention, and when Tommy opened her up the bus disappeared in a mass of black smoke.

The rest of the journey was uneventful until they arrived at Derngate Bus Station. The staff must have been forewarned of this apparition arriving, and David got the passengers off quickly and immediately sent the vehicle to hide down at Houghton Road Works. 'If Aylesbury want it back they can jolly well fetch it themselves. I don't want this **** thing in my bus station!'

Oil on the floor at Derngate caused all sorts of problems. A driver called Jake brought his bus in too quickly and was due to park it facing the back of the restaurant ready to reverse into a bay later on. Unfortunately for Jake, an earlier bus had dropped its oil just inside the entrance door. Jake was able to get the bus facing in the right direction, but could not stop it, and he and his bus joined a party of four enjoying their meal. Fortunately, no one was hurt, although the front of the bus was wrecked and the restaurant wall had to be rebuilt.

David remembers that the last bus out of Derngate was the staff bus. The bus station closed about midnight, and this bus left soon afterwards. However, United Counties cancelled this service soon after David joined and he had a 3-mile walk home at 1.00am.

To cover all the shifts about 350 staff were employed at Derngate, and all the cashing-in was done in a small room above the café. Three Inspectors covered Derngate; one was a Mr Freeman, who was very harsh.

One of David's favourite runs was the 402 to Irthlingborough, as the early run allowed enough time for breakfast at a good little café, followed by two runs down to the Co-op Laundry, then back to Northampton.

On another occasion David and his driver were on an open-backed bus, and David had packed three pushchairs, instead of the regulation two, under the stairs. His driver was in a hurry turning into St Peters Way in Northampton, with the result that the pushchairs flew off the bus and were seen rushing down Gas Street. David stopped his driver and had to sprint after them.

David and another driver went to Silverstone one day. The driver came up behind David as he was talking to a female passenger and pushed him on to her lap. The driver and the lady were friends, so she knew that this would happen.

'Oh, David, what can I do for you?' asked the woman.

'How do you know my name?' said David.

'It's written on your arm,' she replied.

Without him knowing, someone had written his name on the white cuff of his jacket. On returning to Northampton, the driver asked how David had got on with the woman, but his reply is not printable.

Services 321 and 322 visited Quarry Road and Woodside Close in Northampton. One driver achieved the fastest circular run, in 21 minutes. However, he had to wait outside Derngate until the proper time otherwise he would have been shouted at by the Inspector.

At Nether Heyford there is a small hump-backed bridge. On one occasion David and his driver had a 70-seater Bristol FLF. A car was parked on the bridge, and the FLF was too big to go round it. David asked the driver to move, but he refused, stating that he was not going to start it up again, apparently enjoying being a nuisance. However, his face soon changed when the FLF was driven up to his car and gingerly pushed it out of the way.

At Spratton on another occasion David was upstairs collecting fares when the bus did an emergency stop. An RAF plane, with undercarriage down, had hopped over the hedge and missed the bus roof by about a foot. David went forwards and hit the front screen while the passengers all ducked. The noise was horrendous. The driver was sure he was going to be hit and ducked as well.

Ticket machines were mainly Setrights, and each conductor had a numbered machine assigned to him or her. Before each trip the 'tickets sold' number on the back was recorded and the new number recorded at the end of the duty. Each machine counted the number of tickets and the money collected during the shift. If this did not match the number on the back of the machine the conductor had to find the difference. If they did not pay up immediately to balance the amount, it was stopped out of that week's wages.

Finally, David recalls an incident when he was a paperboy and his father Bob was a driver. Bob had bought a second-hand bicycle for David and had painted it up with new stickers. David had taken it out one morning and chained it to a post while he delivered some papers. When he returned the bike

was gone. He finished his round on foot and got into trouble with the newsagent for being late. On arriving home he told his mother all about it, and she called the police. Two detectives arrived, stating that this was a very serious matter and they would try and find the bike. In the meantime, father Bob had been driving his bus near his son's round and had seen a stranger on his son's bike. He forced the bike into the side of the road and remonstrated with the rider, who assured Bob that he had bought the bike for £2 and that it was his. Bob did not believe this and punched the chap, who tumbled down an embankment and ran away.

Bob moved the bike to a safe place and collected it on the way home. When he got home he found the police and pretended to be very angry with his son for being so bad that the police had to be called out. David explained that he had lost his bike and the police heard the whole story from Bob's side. The police then left, followed the bus route and apprehended the thief in Lutterworth. Apparently he was an illegal immigrant and was using the bike to get away from Northampton.

Tony Townsend

Tony was an apprentice at Ideal Motors in Northampton, and at college he was on a course with mainly United Counties apprentices. When he completed his apprenticeship, he was let go and applied to Jock Mitchell at United Counties for a job. He started as a fitter at Northampton Depot in Bedford Road on New Year's Day 1956.

When Tony asked conductress Della to go out with him, she had to pay, as she earned a higher wage; whereas a new conductress was paid £10 19s 9d for a 42-hour week, a new fitter was paid £10 11s 8d. When they went out to the pictures, Della was taken out in style, not in a car but in the company lorry. For a short while she was at Northampton Eye Hospital, next to the back of the Bedford Road Works. To see her, Tony would sign on, go through the works, scale the fuel tanks in the back yard, visit her, then start work. However, when they were married the family transport was the company van. Days out were enjoyed: on Wednesdays they travelled by train to Lowestoft and on Thursdays brought a new Lodekka back to Northampton at a stately 40mph.

Part of Tony's job was to attend road accidents and sort out the mess. One day he was sent up to Kettering Road where an MG sports car had driven under the front of a bus. The driver was still in the car, trapped by the steering wheel. United Counties

A day out with a difference: Tony and Della collect a new Lodekka from Lowestoft. *Tony and Della Townsend collection*

beat the ambulance to the scene, and Tony kept talking to the driver to keep him awake. However, he was so seriously injured that he died as the ambulance crew tried to get him out of the car. This was a traumatic time for all concerned – Tony will never forget this incident.

Tony was also involved in a very well-known Derngate incident. A Bristol KSW left the bus station to go down to the works, but the driver had to avoid another road-user and ended up buried in a building opposite. Tony volunteered to remove the bus.

The speed of coaches was restricted by a device, but some drivers boasted about higher speeds, especially when the M1 motorway opened. The fitters said this was impossible, but they had not counted on the drivers switching the ignition off, which cut off power to the device. Unfortunately, no lights or indicators could be used. This was a very dangerous thing to do.

Della Townsend

Della came to Northampton in the early 1950s. When she wanted to join United Counties she had to have two references, one from a priest and one from a professional person. On New Year's Day 1956 she started as a trainee conductress, and was supposed to have two weeks' training. After one week with a conductress called Maureen, Della was ready to go solo and, after a test, she was passed out by Cyril King. Her first trip was to Raunds on the 403 route. On the way out she felt very sick and realised she was travelsick. However, after some helpful medication she was able to carry on for ten years.

The Inspectors at Derngate Bus Station included Wally and Sam Cockerill and Cyril King, with Norman Maycock as the Depot Superintendent. After training, Della was given her first uniform, and started work with two men, one of whom was Michael Hennessey. Other conductresses were Yvonne Taylor, who later became the company car driver, and Teresa Brennan.

Della remembers the weekend visits to the Swan pub, behind the bus station. In between duties many of the conductresses used to go to the pub. One night a conductress had been drinking, then went out on an open-backed bus. As the bus went round a bollard she fell off into the road. The first the driver knew was when his passengers said that he had left her behind.

Della only recalls one telling-off: Mr Maycock did not approve of her knitted hat, and she was told to remove it.

One year the snow was very heavy and, as no buses ran, passengers were put up in the Bus Station restaurant.

Della at Derngate on the way to Piddington.
Tony and Della Townsend collection

Some of the town journeys were so short, and the buses so crowded, that it could be impossible to issue tickets to all passengers. Top-deck passengers, getting off at British Timken roller bearing works, would hand over the 1½d when they got off. Ticket machines sometimes broke down and emergency tickets had to be issued, which was a tricky job.

Most passengers were not a problem. However, the most troublesome were the young girls from the Notre Dame private school! Della remembers one trip

The Swan Hotel was a local for bus staff at one time. *Roger Warwick collection*

Right: **Brian Buswell 'in the office' before going out on service on a Bristol KSW.** *Brian Buswell collection*

Below: **Preparing for service in front of a newish Lodekka on August Bank Holiday Monday 1957 are (l-r) Brian Buswell, Bert Whitehead, Reg Cox and Bill Bull.** *Brian Buswell collection*

to Brixworth very well. It was the last journey of the day and the bus reversed at Pitsford. Some drunken lads had refused to pay and one pulled a knife on Della, fortunately not using it. She ordered them off at Pitsford, where they hid and attacked the bus when it came out of the

village to pick up a passenger. Della flagged down a car and the driver took her to the nearest police station. The lads were caught.

When the Townsends moved to Stony Stratford, Della retired as a conductress, but later helped out to clean the buses.

Brian Buswell

Brian had two spells with United Counties. His first period was from 1956 to 1964, then later with Stagecoach (United Counties) from 1995 to 2000.

Peter and Joyce Clack

Peter was born at Heaven in Paradise near Gloucester. He joined Bristol Tramways, Gloucester Depot, as a conductor and stayed there a year before being drafted into the Navy in 1943. During the next three years he spent some time in Greek waters, on motor launches, ferrying around the SAS to special operations.

Joyce, in the meantime, had joined the RAF, serving at Innsworth, Gloucester, Malvern – where she first met Peter – Hereford and Boscombe. On leaving the services they got together and moved to Northampton, Joyce's home town.

Peter then joined United Counties and stayed with the company until he retired in 1986. He received awards for long service at 25 years (a gold watch), 35 years (a dinner service), and 45 years (a wall clock), awarded by the later owners of United Counties, Ann Gloag and Brian Souter, in 1988.

Peter was based at Derngate Bus Station and later Greyfriars Bus Station. He was a crew driver and his regular conductor was Ray Wakeling. Ray became involved in the social side of United Counties life and ran the staff club. This raised money for the retired staff outings, children's Christmas parties, food hampers, Christmas presents and other events. The sales of unwanted lost property also helped this fund, and when Ray retired the fund stood at a very healthy £57,000, a credit to him and his team, which included Tommy Guy and Frank Harrison. Some of the dances were held at the Salon in Franklin Gardens.

On the union side, Peter remembers Frank Woska and Bill Morris

Right top to bottom: **Presentations of Peter's long service awards by Fred Dark, Derrick Fytche and Brian Souter.** *All Peter and Joyce Clack collection*

Above: **One of Peter's long service awards.** *Peter and Joyce Clack collection*

United Counties Employees Canteen Fund,
Northampton Depot.

Membership Card.

Member's Signature *P. T. Clack*

G. W. BLUNT,
1 5 NOV 1951   *Managing Secretary*

(later Lord Morris), and Frank Chambers was one of the Driving Examiners at Bedford Road.

Fogs in Northamptonshire could be 'pea-soupers' at times, and gave rise to two incidents that Peter remembers. One day he was on the 401 service to Wellingborough, via Sywell, Mears Ashby and Earls Barton. Coming up the hill into Mears Ashby, he missed the crossroads where he would normally have turned left. He went straight on and slightly to the right, ending up in the farmyard of Mr Stockdale. Realising where he was, his conductor had to see him out and back onto the road again. The other incident concerns a journey on the Brixworth road. Being a big vehicle, the bus was leading about five cars up the main road, again in fog. The cars would not overtake and followed like sheep. When he got to Pitsford, the route entered the village, reversed and came out again. The cars followed and there was great fun while they all sorted themselves out at the reversing point.

Northampton Corporation buses would sometimes cease running in the fog, leaving the United Counties buses to carry on. Passengers would be carried to bus stops not normally used; some people would start walking and buses would pick them up on the way home.

At Derngate Peter worked for Norman Maycock, who was a strict boss but fair. Later he worked for Rod Davies, and found him a good boss also. The most important person to the drivers and conductors was the wages clerk, who made sure the wages were correct. In Peter's time the clerk was Mrs Parker.

Peter remembers two amusing incidents out of many at Derngate and out on the road. One driver, Les Bree, found a boy's school cap on his bus. He rolled up his trousers, put on the cap and slumped down in his driving seat. The passengers thought he really was a schoolboy and refused to travel until he took the cap off and rolled his trousers back down. On another occasion, when two buses met in a village, the drivers got out and had a pretend prize-fight in the middle of the street. The passengers did not realise it was staged and watched in amazement.

Peter did not have many breakdowns on his travels. However, he remembers once that the throttle cable broke and he had to use a piece of string instead. He also had an accelerator pedal stick down, so he could not control his speed. Luckily, the pedal righted itself before Peter hit anything. One day he drove a vehicle into a hole in the road while overtaking another bus; the road was narrow and one of the bus's wheels went down the hole. Embarrassingly, the bus was stuck there for a few hours before rescue came, but a local inhabitant supplied everyone with tea and food.

Children from Uppingham School used to be conveyed to and from the station and their homes, on one occasion by seven buses. Peter and several others were waiting for the delayed train and went into a pub.

Above: **Peter Clack with a 1933 TD2 on private hire.** *Peter and Joyce Clack collection*

Below: **Peter sometimes took his family on day excursions. In the first picture he is at Longleat, and in the second with daughters Alyson and Fiona at Cheddar.** *Peter and Joyce Clack collection*

Unfortunately for them, Norman Maycock came to check the operation and found them in the pub. They should have been suspended, but were let off with a caution. Two others on this run were Ray Fall and Stan Armstrong.

Peter found that the gearboxes on some of the buses were easy to use, while others were hard. In some cases he found that the gears seemed to have moved since the last time he used them. Also, some of the buses were so hard to manoeuvre that he had to stand up to pull the wheel round. Some of the double-deckers were called 'Scharnhorsts', after the Second World War German battleship, as they were bulky and hard to drive.

In Peter's early career, all buses going down Victoria Promenade had to be single-deckers or 'Saloons', due to the low bridge carrying the railway to Bedford out of St John's station at the bottom of Guildhall Road. This station had closed in 1939, and the bridge was eventually demolished, enabling double-deckers to be used. Some bridges carried canals over country roads and one or two were so low that even some single-deckers could only go under them

with care; if they had a raised destination box on the roof they were banned, as on the 316 route to Ashby St Ledgers.

Later in his career Peter drove coaches on the regular Nottingham to London routes and summer excursions, including his first journey up the newly constructed M1 motorway with fellow driver Tommy Read. As Peter was from Gloucestershire he was sent on the trips to the Wye Valley and Cheddar Gorge, but his favourite trip was to Matlock and Derby.

Peter had a trick when driving long distances on

Right: **Peter and Fiona on the tree-lopper in 1980.** *Peter and Joyce Clack collection*

Below: **Tree-lopping bus 620 LFM goes out on patrol, being waved off by well-wishers! The Derngate Bus Station restaurant is on the left and the booking office on the right.** *Peter and Joyce Clack collection*

The last Northampton crews (drivers and conductors) retired in the 1970s. Seen here are, on the back row, Terry Sweeney, Michael Lewis, Jeffrey Fairman and Raymond Wakeling, and on the front row Raymond Neal, Dorothy Page, John Machin and Peter Clack. *Northampton Chronicle & Echo*

motorways. To ease his foot, he used to put a brick on the accelerator and place his foot on top. If he needed to brake suddenly, he was able to kick the brick away.

When United Counties moved to Greyfriars Bus Station, Peter and John Merrifield were asked to help clear out the old offices. In doing so he found that Norman Maycock had left his salt dish behind on retirement – he had used it to rest his pipe on. Peter saved it from being thrown away and proudly displays it as a remembrance of Mr Maycock.

The post of vehicle dispatcher came up at Northampton, and Norman asked Peter to do it, for which he was paid a shilling extra an hour. After a while he became so fed up that he asked to go back to driving, and Henry Hall took over the dispatching job. However, before he left he had one or two funny moments. One driver was not happy with the bus he had been allocated. Peter told him the only other bus was the one behind him. That turned out to be

without wheels, and the driver had to use what he had been given. The other occasion was when Peter was under pressure from Norman for another bus – all serviceable buses were out and none were coming out of the works. Peter's only alternative was to draw a bus on a piece of paper, which he gave to Norman. He was not amused. From those days Peter remembers Inspectors Hurnell and (Ginger) Freeman, Mr Doughty, a fitter in the garage, and Tim Kelly, who worked for United Counties.

Another job that Peter did was to help out on the tree-lopper, which at the time was former service bus 620 LFM. The bus covered all the company area, and for about three months was based at Northampton. Peter used to go out with colleagues on all routes in the Northampton and Stony Stratford Depot areas. The cuttings should have been taken to local landfill sites, but on many occasions bonfires were lit on the sides of roads. In those days the Stony Stratford area included what was to become Milton Keynes, which was then a small village with a small local sub-garage at Bletchley, Tavistock Street. Tree-lopping duties were 9.00am to 5.00pm, and Peter found the money was less than driving split shifts and Joyce could not get used to Peter having regular hours. Sometimes the family used to go and help.

John Merrifield and Peter had another job at Stony Stratford. Milton Keynes city services were just

starting and they were sent out to erect the bus stops.
They bought or made their own equipment and used
to keep it on the tree-lopper. When they finished and
went back to driving, the equipment went home, and
the new crew had to find other equipment as a result.

The bus profession is carrying on in the family, as
one of Peter and Joyce's sons is now a Supervisor for
First Bus in Northampton.

Doug Freeman

Doug Freeman was a conductor, driver and Inspector
at Derngate. He started with United Counties in
1956 and left in 1986. He was then taken on by
Northampton Corporation, where he worked until
retiring in 1995. His boss at United Counties was
District Superintendent Norman Maycock.

Madge Halton

When Madge Halton left school she took up an
apprenticeship at Leal & Toyer, dressmakers, then
spent time at Smith's dressmakers. During the war she
was called up and became a member of the WAAF,
mainly employed at RAF Watnell near Nottingham.

On being demobbed Madge returned to
Northampton. She went to the Derngate Bus Station
Café with her mother and son one day in 1949.
The Manageress was a Mrs Appleton, and one of
her cashiers was off sick, so she offered Madge a

Top: **Northampton's Derngate Bus Station Café
entrance as built in the 1930s.** *Roger Warwick
collection*

Middle: **The Café after refurbishment while Mrs
Halton was in charge.** *Roger Warwick collection*

Below: **Celebrity visitor: the Café Manageress,
American actor Ben Lyon, one of the waitresses,
and Bebe Daniels (Mrs Lyon) in the Derngate
Café in 1938.** *Northampton Chronicle & Echo*

temporary job. This temporary job lasted 27 years until Derngate Bus Station was closed and the café demolished.

The cashier's office was by the door, with the cigarette and chocolate counters next to it. The Café's Snack Bar, toilets and kitchens made up the bus station's internal wall, while the roadside wall was windowed throughout its length. Many of the customers preferred seats and waitresses, and there was room in the Café for 100 customers at any one time, and some lunchtimes 200 meals were provided. The corner by the bus station entrance door was named 'Pets Corner', and was used mainly by the officers of the company. The first General Manager was Mr Pittard, then others included Mr Robinson, Mr Wood, Teddy Dravers and Colin Clubb. Mr Wood seemed to take more interest in the Café than other General Managers. This included kitting out the waiting staff with black dresses; later the uniform included green dresses. When Mr Wood died Madge and her team catered at his funeral by request of the family. In the early days the Manageress did not qualify for a company pension, but Mr Robinson changed this policy. The offices above the Café were rented out to an architect.

When Mrs Appleton became Mrs Carol and resigned her post, Madge was appointed as her replacement. She went to Northampton Technical College for a day-release catering course. Her job was supervised by the General Manager, while Madge supervised about 20 staff, including kitchen staff, waitresses, Snack Bar staff (in the bus station itself), chocolate and cigarette counter staff, and cashiers.

Opposite bottom and top right: **The Café Snack Bar and the chocolate and cigarette counter, with Rose Moore at the cash till.** *Both Madge Halton collection*

Middle: **The chocolate and cigarette counter, with Madge Halton and Diana Ramscar.** *Madge Halton collection*

Right: **Dolly Coles, Dorothy Essery, Rosaline Brown, Jane Johnson, Madge Halton, Reggie Cox, Mary Scott, Eveline Sawkins and Annie Perrins where all present at the** end of the Derngate Café. *Northampton Chronicle & Echo, Madge Halton collection*

During factory fortnight, other holidays and on Saturdays, students would help out, some of whom came back time and time again.

The Café was a meeting place for the influential and well-groomed of Northampton, including the officers of the company and members of the local Rotary Club. Actors from the adjacent Royal Theatre Repertory Company would also come in for lunch while learning their lines; these included the now well-known Lionel Blair, Helen Worth, Adam Faith and John Bird.

At coffee time the Café was packed. Coffee cost 4d a cup, and when the price was increased to 4½d one solicitor refused to come in. However, he did come in on the last day, as he had been a regular for so many years before.

In the early days the Café opened at 9.00am and closed at 10.00pm, Monday to Saturday. On Saturday nights a special 5-shilling dinner of soup, roast chicken and all the trimmings, sweet and coffee was provided; bookings were taken, as this service was very popular. In later years the number of evening meals

Above right: **The first version of the Snack Bar, photographed in April 1963.** *Northampton Chronicle & Echo*

Below: **The bus station Snack Bar, second version.** *Roger Warwick collection*

reduced and the closing time was brought forward to 7.00pm. Staff were hard to find for late rotas on a Saturday.

By comparison, Derngate Bus Station's Snack Bar was so popular that it was open seven days a week, and Madge and her assistant, Diana Ramscar, would have to help out on some Sundays. In the early days queues for the Booking Office, on a summer Saturday, would be all the way along Derngate and up St Giles Street. In the summer the Café became very hot and the windows on the road side did not open, although those on the Booking Office and bus station side did.

Fish for the Café was sourced from a local fishmonger, meat from a local butcher and vegetables from a local greengrocer, and milk was also local.

Madge had a card for the local cash and carry, Linnells, for all the consumables. The most popular dish was shepherd's pie, which was famous throughout the town. Other popular dishes included haddock and chips, and the daily roast. (Angela Seelig, 'Joe' Beckett's granddaughter, remembers being taken to the Café for Saturday lunch by her grandparents. Her favourite meal was fish fingers and chips.)

A bus was provided to bring office staff up from the Bedford Road offices and works for lunch at the Café; the office dinner hour was 1.40 to 2.40pm. If the staff bus was not available, the Bedford bus made an additional stop at Bedford Road; the Yardley Hastings staff were usually quite helpful in this respect. Office staff from the booking office at Derngate also used the Café. One of these was a shy youngster named Roger Warwick, and staff at the Café used to tease the youngster mercilessly. Road staff and Inspectors had their own canteen. The managers here were George Blunt and later Doreen Palmer; Mr Palmer worked in the Cash Office above the Booking Office. The Café accounts were done by staff at Bedford Road, and internal auditors would check the accounts of all food establishments.

Madge was responsible for providing buffet meals for meetings in the Board Room at Bedford Road. Food was prepared at the Café and taken down in Madge's car, which was kept at a nearby Albion Place house, owned by United Counties. The Café also did the catering for visits from local and national dignitaries, including Norman Fowler MP and NBC Chairperson Mr Niblock. The latter was so impressed that he offered coffee to Madge and her colleagues when they later visited a Catering Exhibition in London.

Coach parties sometimes used the café. One party took all the cutlery away with them; Madge found an Inspector who went on the coach and got it all back. Most coach passengers only had a few minutes at Northampton, so used the Snack Bar for sandwiches and coffee.

One customer, a well-heeled lady from Bedford Mansions, opposite the bus station, used to come in each day and take a teaspoon home with her. The cutlery was easy to distinguish as it was initially stamped 'Derngate Café'. Similarly, each week a lady from Broughton used to come into town to do her shopping. Coming into the Café just after it opened, she used the toilets and took the soap home with her. To stop this the soap was not put out until she had left.

In 1976 Madge and her team were made redundant, as there was to be no café at the new bus station at Greyfriars. For the last four years of her employment she became the Canteen Liaison Officer for the company, with a desk in one of the Engineering Offices with Ted Vickery. Madge now looked after all the canteens owned by the company and a new one opened in the works, run by Doreen Palmer. This job entailed travelling to all the company depots and bus stations to check any problems with the managers/manageresses.

Top: **Madge Halton receives her 25-year certificate and clock from Bob Rawlinson.** *Madge Halton collection*

Middle **The Engineering Office staff, including Yvonne, Eunice, Ted Vickery, Madge Halton, Peggy Jarrett, Sylvia, Rance Muscutt, Jenny and Janet.** *Madge Halton collection*

Above: **Frank Phillips and Madge Halton on her retirement.** *Northampton Chronicle & Echo, Madge Halton collection*

Madge and Rethe Cherry were great friends and still keep in touch. Madge used to attend company dinners, mainly held at the Salon in Franklin Gardens. At one of these Mr Howcroft sang an impromptu song and surprised everyone. Madge retired in 1980, and still lives in Northampton.

The following article was written by Jane Bakowski, a reporter at the *Chronicle & Echo*:

Goodbye shepherd's pie, farewell spotted dick

There is an old lady who sits in a certain corner of the Derngate Restaurant, Northampton, every day. She goes in for coffee around eleven and stays peacefully chatting and looking out of the window until it is time for lunch. 'There is no point in going home,' she explained. 'I'd only have to turn round and come straight back again.' Daisy, as the staff call her, is just one of the restaurant's regular customers. She has been going there since 1937, the year after it opened.

But when the last person leaves Derngate, it will be closing its doors for good. For the march of progress has at last overtaken one of Northampton's best-loved institutions and now that the new Bus Station is coming into operation, United Counties' only restaurant has become redundant.

Few of the old regulars were surprised by the news, but still their reaction is of deep concern. For the Derngate is far more than simply a restaurant. 'It has always been used as a club, where you could meet your friends and not be hurried by anyone,' said Miss Dorothy Foyle, a customer of 30 years standing.

The peculiar charm of the place has attracted a wide range of faithful customers. Bank managers and solicitors lunch there, old people meet for coffee and a chat, generations of local schoolgirls have enjoyed illicit snacks in the far corner and every day mothers haul in armfuls of shopping and children for a moment's brief respite. On Saturdays, farmers from all corners of the county take in their families for lunch after a morning at the cattle market.

The secret of the Derngate, with its sensible tiled floors and Formica-topped tables, its plastic tulips and mock stone wallpaper, and its very serviceable crockery, is something apart from all these things. It is quite simply its friendliness.

'When you are talking about the Derngate, you are talking about the people,' said Mrs Gillian Elmer, who has been visiting the restaurant since she was a schoolgirl. 'It is a part of my life, and I have always been welcome here.'

Mrs Elmer pointed out the table where her father, England cricketer V. W. C. Jupp, used to sit.

'It really became an offshoot of the George Row Club here during the war, with all the men hiding behind their *Financial Times*. But all through the years it was something tremendously solid to cling to.' This solidarity remains and is treasured by Derngate customers. There is space to relax and the time to sit and watch the world go by. Above all, there is a welcome you can be sure about.

Waitress Mrs Mary Scott has been working there for 21 years. For her, its closing is almost unbelievable. Like many of the staff, she has a special relationship with her customers, built up over many years. The waitresses move to different tables each week, but their regulars faithfully follow them around. 'I can't help getting involved with people – they are more like friends,' said Mary. 'Sometimes I think I ought to open up an advice bureau!'

The Derngate menu, like the customers, rarely changes. It is good, honest, home-cooking – and plenty of it – with shepherd's pie, roast beef and spotted dick the perennial favourites.

Miss Evelyn Sawkins, the Cook, joined the staff in 1939, when she was just 15. 'I was only the washer-up then, but I was called up in 1942, and while I was in the forces I learned a lot about cookery.'

On her return in 1946, Miss Sawkins started to produce the kind of hearty meals for which the restaurant – and, incidentally, the Army – is famous.

'Well,' said one old lady, 'you can only get things like egg and chips elsewhere, and you don't call that a proper dinner, do you?'

Manageress Mrs Madge Halton has spent half a lifetime at the Derngate. 'You see children grow up, become courting couples, and then come in with children of their own.'

Mary Scott's characteristic concern for her customers overrides even her own feelings of dismay at the Derngate closure. 'There are old people who leave here on Saturday and don't speak to anyone else until they come back on Monday. And what about the bachelors who come here? A lot of them don't know how to boil an egg – whatever will they do?'

Mary knows which of her regulars like weak coffee and the ones who like plenty of gravy on their pie or small helpings of custard. 'Often we have people with friends or relatives who are in the General Hospital after accidents. We say, "Sit here a while and have some tea," and strangers are always pleased and surprised.'

Over the decades, the Derngate has developed a style and an atmosphere that is all its own. None of the regulars is sure where they will go when it closes for, as Mary Scott said, 'You try and find another Derngate!'

But one thing is certain: the Derngate Café has become as much a part of life for so many people that it will not be forgotten. After all, who else can make spotted dick like Eveline Sawkins?

An unnamed customer subsequently wrote to the *Chronicle & Echo*:

Not many bus station cafés, I fancy, can call themselves real social centres of their respective towns and yet that is exactly what the Derngate Café, at Northampton, is. I have been going into it now for many years and it's amazing how many of the key people of the town and district you meet there.

Town Councillors, Civic Officials, Repertory Theatre actors, authors, journalists, people prominent in all walks of life, from professional sportsmen and solicitors to well-known businessmen and artists. You see them all here sooner or later.

Ideally situated at the front of the United Counties large covered station, the Derngate is renowned for miles around for its reasonable prices, quick service, and excellent table and snack bar facilities. In fact, I don't really know what I should do without the Derngate. The staff and very well-known manageress, who has been here for 22 years, have set a standard in whatever you order, which I personally have found always maintained

There is a full lunch menu (changed daily) available from midday, and right up to closing time, at 6.45pm, you can get a complete service of grills and light refreshments, such as gammon steak, egg and chips, plaice and chips, chicken salads, omelettes, etc.

I go in a lot for tea (the teacakes and home-made scones are especially good, positively overflowing with butter), and if I'm late I can always get a very good high tea. Ham and chips, for example. The salads are extremely nice also, and if you want a quick meal before rushing off to catch your bus there's always a variety of rolls, pies and cakes at the bar.

The café opens at 10.00am each morning (closed Sundays, by the way) and I'm usually one of the first for coffee or a cup of tea. It's one of the largest cafés in Northampton, and though the town has a number of very good restaurants the Derngate is perhaps the only one to which the term 'indispensable' could really be applied.

Elsie Thomas

Elsie's son Bill tells us that his mother worked at the Derngate Café as a waitress. She looked after about 8-10 tables and had her own regular customers; if they could not get on one of her tables, they would be upset. The Manageress then was a Lilly Bret.

One of Elsie's regulars was Lionel Blair, who at the time was working at either the New Theatre or the Rep. At that time he was not very well off and used to come in for a cup of tea only; he said he could not afford anything else. Elsie used to feel sorry for him and would bring a couple of buttered scones as well – who paid for them no one knows. Lionel Blair went on to become an accomplished tap dancer and made his name on television and stage. He can now afford tea and scones.

Another regular customer was the mother of Marcia Falkender, who worked in 10 Downing Street, then as Personal Assistant to Harold Wilson when he was Prime Minister. Northampton cricketer Colin Milburn, was another regular. He unfortunately had

to give up cricket when he lost an eye. However, he set up a sports shop in the town and was still seen in the Café.

Bill knew a young lad called Des O'Connor, who played football for Northampton Town, worked at Church's shoe factory and later for United Counties twice, once on the road and once in the office. Both boys used to go to the Roadmenders Club. Des subsequently went on to better things on television and stage, and at the time of writing hosts TV's *Countdown*.

George Hawkins

George spent a year training at Head Office in Northampton, working in schedules, publicity (with Mr Whiteley) and road service (with Bob Coote). He remembers working with Roger Warwick, and that the Traffic Manager and his assistant had offices to the right of the reception area, while the General Manager was on the left. The Traffic Office was on the other side of the corridor on the right. Only visitors and the General Manager were allowed in through the front door; others had to use the entrances at the side and rear of the depot and works. While at Head Office George was in digs next door in Vigo Cottages with one of the managers.

While there he remembers that half the Northampton bus fleet were housed in Bedford Road, with the remainder at Derngate Bus Station.

Northampton Bedford Road Depot, with the Head Office to the left. *Roger Warwick collection*

One coach driver he remembers was Len Bull.

He recalls that the staff at Welford outstation were a law unto themselves. On a Saturday a double-decker came out from Northampton, and as the crews only worked this once every two years they could not remember their way into one village. At the crossroads the bus might come from any one of four directions, so as a result a lad from the village was sent up a tree to see which way it was coming, and the passengers then stood on the correct road.

Tom Kehoe

Tom was the oldest of three living on a farm in Ireland, which had 14 sheep and some fattening pigs. Tom had a choice of taking over the farm or going to England with his fiancée.

Above right: **A young Tom Kehoe, on the extreme right, with Jack Hartley, Frank Johnson, Stan Morris and two others.** *Tom Kehoe collection*

Right: **Norman Maycock presents Bill Mills with his retirement present, watched by colleagues (l-r) Martin Kelly, Roy Burdett and Malcolm Cox.** *Tom Kehoe collection*

After selling the pigs, he left in a taxi and headed off for Northampton in 1961, where they stayed with Martin

Kelly and his family.

Finding a job at Northampton Brewery, Tom stuck his nose in the building but did not enter, as he could not stand the sweet smell of the brew. He then tried the fire service, but did not like the look of that either. Eventually he settled for a life on the buses.

Tom was taught to conduct by Cyril Farmer at the training school. His first turn of duty was under supervision on the 302 service to Moulton; he collected the fares while Cyril sorted out the door and rang the bell. Tom was very nervous but overcame this in time and enjoyed the job.

Tom was the last person to be tested for driving by 'Joe' Beckett, before Joe became an examiner. He worked at Northampton for Norman Maycock, who was a hard but fair man at work, but would be completely different out of work. At work Tom would just get a nod, but elsewhere Norman would be friendly and chatty, even standing a round of drinks.

In 1976 Tom entered the United Counties heat of Driver of the Year, at Bedford. He did well, but did not get to the finals. Buses were backed up to a false wall – the nearer to the wall, the more points were scored. Other manoeuvres were through rugby-type posts, which were increasingly moved nearer together and the headroom reduced until the driver touched them.

Tom recalls that machines had not been installed on some of the OMO buses, so an honesty box was fitted instead. Money was paid in the

same, but tickets were not issued.

He remembers that Fred Archer was a very good union representative, being a Branch Secretary for the TGWU. Unfortunately he was killed by a drunken car driver. His greatest union achievement was to get the Spreadover Rate from £10.40 to £20.00 per week.

On a Sunday the last buses to Daventry changed crews at Weedon,

Top: **A presentation, including, on the front row, Peter Westley, Barry Warner, Roy Burdett, Mick Mullins and Tom Kehoe. Second from right on the back row is Frank Hutchins.** *Tom Kehoe collection*

Middle: **Another presentation: on the back row are Tony Cox, Bill Lawrence, Keith Kidson, Ray Ramsey, Barry Warner, Dave Parker, Tom Kehoe and Ben Colson, and on the front row Barry Hinkley, Roy Burdett and Mick Mullins.** *Tom Kehoe collection*

Bottom: **Here the back row includes Tom Kehoe, Rod Davies, Richard Askew, Mick Dunn, Michelle Hargreaves and Alex Carter. On the front row are Mick Mullins, Richard Van Hoof, Mick Cornwall and Ray Ramsey.** *Tom Kehoe collection*

Below: **Former Kettering driver Fred Moore organised coach trips, and on one of them are Tom and his wife and two former colleagues enjoying a rough boat crossing.** *Tom Kehoe collection*

Friends Malcolm Cox and Martin Kelly with their wives at an awards ceremony. *Tom Kehoe collection*

Pat Deane, Frank Duffy, Geoff Heginbotham and Tom Kehoe with colleague Rodney Dawe. *Northampton Chronicle & Echo*

the Stony Stratford ones at Stoke Bruerne, and the Bedford buses at Yardley Hastings.

Tom was involved in other jobs at times. He used to take his turn on the tree-lopper. The smaller branches were taken to a lay-by at Quinton for burning, while the larger ones were logged up for the landlady at a pub in Old. When required Tom would also take out the 'Caravan' and relocate bus stops or put out new ones.

Tom retired in the early 2000s and now works hard in his garden producing plants for the local church. In 2007-08 he and his friends spent eight months organising a well-attended Derngate Reunion at Northampton Working Men's Club. Tom's brother Frank, who was also on the buses, had hoped to go to the reunion, but sadly he died just before the event, which was a great disappointment for all the family.

Clive Perryman

Clive worked as a conductor and driver at Derngate and Greyfriars bus stations, and Mrs Perryman's Auntie Molly used to work in the Café at Derngate, as a waitress.

Clive remembers that the bays at Derngate had to be reversed into. One day Peter Clack and Jeff Firman each tried to get a bus into the same bay at the same time; each approached from a different direction and suffered a coming together. Norman Maycock asked who got there first and the replies indicated that it had been a dead heat.

Clive Perryman and Frank Sullivan pose before leaving Derngate Bus Station for the last time on 1 May 1976. *W. J. S. Meredith, Clive Perryman collection*

Above: Bay 9 is on the extreme right of this photograph. The Inspectors' Office was next to the coach bays on the left, and the canteen was upstairs, between the bus and coach bays. *Roger Warwick collection*

Middle: The Welford bus in the ditch. The road had to be closed to recover the bus. *Clive Perryman collection*

Below right: An on-hire Eastern National double-decker coach leaves Derngate Bus Station. The main offices were above the travel shop by the vehicle exit and the passenger entrance to the left of this. The Café is on the extreme left, and in the distance, beyond the Swan Hotel on the left, is Northampton's Guildhall. *Trevor Turner collection*

Clive was out in the snow one day, going to Corby. He was confused when he got back, as he had arrived 1½ hours late, but was reported by Inspector Frank Cox for running early.

Clive remembers that the Silverstone crew were Fred Mortimer and Arthur Rush, while Charlie Cox was a conductor from Yardley Hastings. The last buses on the 128 crossed at Yardley and the crews changed. Others he remembers are Tommy Kerr, who went down to Bedford Road as a repairer of the Setright machines, Ray (a driver/Inspector), Colin Needle, Ray Neal and Graham Neale (at the depot), and Inspectors Doug Freeman and Tom Smith.

'In the pink' during a charity event are Tony Cox, Michelle Hargreaves and Sandra Cripps, with Clive Perryman in the long pink wig. *Clive Perryman collection*

During their time at Derngate the spare staff used to hang about Bay 9. One day a bus backed into the bay, filled with passengers, then rolled away on its own – the driver had left the handbrake off. One of the spare drivers jumped in and stopped it. Several buses also ran away and into the back of the Café, mainly due to oil on the floor. Even when a barrier was put up, it still used to happen.

One day Clive and Peter Dempsey were on the last turn back empty from Welford when their Bristol FS bus wobbled off the road and into a ditch. Peter was distracted and Clive lost all the change he was checking around the ground floor of the bus. Stunned by the accident, Clive left by the emergency exit and fell into the ditch. Both driver and conductor were shaken by the experience and were transported back home by about 1.00am. The bus did not make it home until the next day.

Another accident occurred at Flore, on bad bends on the A45. Alan Burns ('Medallion Man') was driving round the bend when he was hit by a lorry coming the other way. He was lucky to survive as the lorry drove straight through the cab.

The bus people's watering hole was the Swan public house, later The Mailcoach. When on breaks, staff could be found propping up the bar, and the Inspectors knew where to find them.

During his driving career Clive worked with Frank Sullivan on private hires. Several were to children's adventure camps in Wales and the West Country.

Sometimes he meets these children as adults and they still remember the trips. He enjoyed driving the Leyland Leopard coaches best. One set of children clubbed together and bought him a cut-glass bonbon jar and left in it a message for him as a thanks.

One regular United Counties coach service was to Heathrow. On one occasion Clive was accused of stealing cases belonging to passengers when he offered to help them.

On the day that Derngate Bus Station closed, Clive was on a late turn with his conductor Frank Sullivan, and the Inspector told them that they were taking the last bus out on service 321. The bus had a notice in the front window and a small wreath over the window, and was photographed by local enthusiasts. The next day was even busier. All the vehicles had to be relocated to Greyfriars, and the excess to Northampton Corporation Depot at St James.

When later working for Stagecoach, Clive was at the Guilsborough outstation; he drove the Guilsborough bus but was based at Northampton, which he found all very strange. Due to ill health Clive then moved to cleaning buses, steam-cleaning, driving the recovery lorry and fuelling buses. Later he became the main Helpline person and worked at Rothersthorpe Avenue. He retired at the end of November 2007 and at the time of writing works part-time for a skip firm. One of his last jobs was to help raise money for the Breast Cancer Charity as part of the Head Office team.

Jean Warwick

Jean married Roger Warwick and worked at the Head Office at Houghton Road from 1956 to 1963, then transferred to Derngate Bus Station, and to Greyfriars Bus Station when it opened in 1976. She describes herself as a general clerk working on mileages and all the usual variety of work at a Depot Office and Head Office. At Derngate and Greyfriars she worked in the Express Department and liaised with Head Office at Houghton Road and with other Express offices.

Pete Wedgebrow

Pete worked for the company from 1970 to about 1984. He worked as a shift fitter whilst he was at Northampton Depot in Houghton Road and remembers that one of his jobs was to go up to Derngate Bus Station to check and fuel any buses there. He also had to transfer vehicles from the depot and works up to Derngate.

He remembers one night at 1.00am going up to Derngate with a KSW and skidding on oil on the bus station floor, completing a full circle without hitting anything.

In about 1980 Pete moved on to Wellingborough Depot and was the charge fitter there. He left two years before the depot closed in 1986.

Pete owns a bench from Derngate Bus Station. Apparently when the bus station was being demolished unwanted items started to appear in many houses, gardens and garages.

Janet Palmer

Janet worked as one of a team of six at the Derngate staff canteen. She was there for four years, and Mr Mason was in charge.

The Derngate Canteen Liaison Committee: E. Stock, Ray Wakeling, G. Fenton, Norman Maycock, M. Doyle, Janet Palmer and S. Winferah. *NBC News*

Jenny and David Britten

Jenny worked for United Counties as a conductress and David as a driver in the 1960s and early 1970s.

Staff shortages on Saturday afternoons and evenings were so acute that United Counties used to employ its own office staff and outside part-time workers to run the buses. Jenny and her husband worked for other companies on Monday to Friday and on the buses on a Saturday.

In 1972 United Counties started to transfer all buses to One Person Operation, which meant that part-timers were no longer required as often as before. Jenny and David both enjoyed their time on the buses and remember those days with affection.

David Blackburn

Although David never worked for United Counties, he was a passenger for many years. He says that he was spoiled by having lived in London; when he came to Northampton in 1944 he found that the frequency of the bus services was different from what he was used to.

He lived in Far Cotton and tried to go to town on the bus, but was told that, due to local agreements with Northampton Corporation Transport, he would have to buy a worker's season ticket if he wished to travel on a United Counties bus.

Later he moved to Cold Ashby, through which buses went on their way to Welford. Unfortunately, they came into the village and straight out without picking up any waiting passengers.

Jean Warwick at a presentation. *Gordon Smith collection*

Jenny Britten between runs with Bristol RELL 330. *Jenny Britten collection*

Frank Duffy

Frank worked as a driver at United Counties and Stagecoach East. His claim to fame is appearing in the *Chronicle & Echo* in 1980 being served with tea by his colleague Les Smith, as can be seen in the accompanying photo.

John Pratt

John worked in the schedules office at Head Office from 1947 to 1952. Using graphs, he worked out work schedules for buses and staff. He was one of the first staff to use the graph system, which is still in use at the time of writing.

Frank Duffy is in the background of this 1980 photograph. Also present that day were Bob Brown, Jeff Fairman, John Machin, Pat Deane and Danny Kerr. *Northampton Chronicle & Echo*

Frank Duffy is seen again on the extreme right at the Safe Driving awards. Others present were Geoff Heginbotham, Bob George, Bill Nicholson, Les Jones, H. Barnes, Roy Burdett, Frank Johnson, Mick Mullins, Martin Kelly, Fred Archer, Colin Clubb, Tom Kehoe, Stan Lilford, J. Smart and K. Chesterfield. *Tom Kehoe collection*

He remembers that some of the Spreadover Work was based on three times 2-hour shifts at breakfast, lunch and tea, and that the extra payment was 1s 6d a day. At that time Northampton Depot had 30 double-deckers, and he remembers an Inspector Waterman, General Manager Reg Pritchard, Traffic Manager Reg Howe, and a Mr White. His boss was Jack Hartley, and other colleagues were Alf Knight, Johnny Bunce and a Miss Adams, who did the private hire work. Mr Taylor dealt with the ticket clippings from the Willibrew tickets, Bill Goodman was the company artist, and Mr Spice used to make the bus announcements at Derngate Bus Station and worked in the publicity department. Up the stairs were Doug Neale and Mr Rolfe, the Company Secretary. Fred Merriman came later to take over that role.

When John was at Bedford Road an Eastern National bus passed the office going to Bedford. Eastern National did not use Derngate but started its services in Victoria Promenade.

Northampton had outstations at Long Buckby, Welford and Silverstone in the late 1940s and early 1950s. Parcels were collected and delivered by bus to and from local public houses and shops, and timetables included hospital visiting hours and market days.

The last bus from and to Stony Stratford was about 9.00pm, and the drivers used to meet half way and change over, allowing both of them to get home earlier. The buses would stay at the wrong depot for the night then go home next day. However, if either crew wanted to keep their bus and take it back home, the passengers swapped over instead.

Kevin Fitchett

Kevin worked at United Counties for 12 years after leaving school in 1976. His first job was as the post boy, one of his jobs being to collect all the post suitcases from the early morning buses from the depots. Later in the day he had to collect up the outgoing mail and distribute it around the buses to go back to the depots. He would catch a ride with a post bus to Bedford Road Depot and distribute the post there; the bus would wait for him and take him back to Derngate. The last job of the day was to go and see Miss Cherry and collect the General Manager's post, which always seemed to be in a rush to be out.

In 1978 Kevin moved to the Central Works and became the mechanic on the company's Setright ticket machines. He had three different types: one was a small machine, another was larger and the third was the electronic version. For this job he had a pay rise from £27.00 to £63.00 a week. Luton Depot used Almex ticket machines, which were left over from Luton Corporation days.

Kevin remembers Ray Ramsey, Roger and Jeannie Warwick, Bob Whiteley and Tom White (who had a job for life). Mr Maycock was very strict and used to smoke a pipe. Miss Piercy was in the Ticket Audit Section and the staff were afraid of her!

Kevin remembers that one of the drivers was called 'Foggy' Warwick (he was not related to Roger and Jeannie). He got his nickname from getting lost on the Roade bus at Ashton and ending up in a field. Another time he took a wrong turning and ended up on the M1 motorway, which was under construction at the time; luckily he was able to go back the way he had come.

Kevin remembers that some conductors became used to drilling the counters on the machines to fiddle the money; they also used to glue up the machines for the same reason.

Kevin occasionally covered for clerks in other areas, sometimes for Val Everard at Wellingborough and Mrs Bell at Luton. After leaving United Counties he became a police officer.

Peter Lovell

Peter's father George Lovell worked for local company, Syd Kingston Bus Services, operating from Silverstone to Northampton. United Counties bought this company in about 1934 and many of the staff operated the service 345 for United Counties thereafter. One of the Kingston crews was made up of Mr Kingston and Mr Mortimer, and Mrs Kingston was the conductress on Wednesdays and Saturdays.

Peter also remembers Freddy Reeve, who was George's conductor, Arthur Rush, another conductor, drivers Ron Rogers, Fred Snelson and Brian Dale, and Syd Lovell, another driver but no relation to George. Peter's father worked for the company for more than 38 years as his medal shows; the first was awarded in 1949.

When George retired he was given a lunch with other retirees at Northampton.

Steve and Tom Diggin

Both Steve and Tom worked for United Counties at Northampton; Steve started as a conductor in 1960 and Tom in 1977.

In 1962 the driver trainer was a Mr Horn, and 'Joe' Beckett examined Steve. He passed, and the bus used was Bristol KSW 929 JBD 966. His first run was on

Above: **George Lovell and friend with Syd Kingston's bus in the background.** *Peter Lovell collection*

Top left: **The Syd Kingston depot at Silverstone, later used by United Counties.** *Roger Warwick collection*

Left: **Bristol LWL 411 on the 345 service at Cattle End, Silverstone.** *Peter Lovell collection*

Below: **George's medals.** *Peter Lovell collection*

the same day, taking the 5.35pm to
Lower Heyford with Reg Holton
as conductor. Steve also remembers
driver Nobby Clarke from 1961.

The one trip Steve always
dreaded was to the far-flung wilds
of Raunds – it seemed to take for
ever to get there and back. Steve also
visited a field in the fog, at Ashton.

Steve left United Counties in
1967 and went to work for Northampton Corporation
Transport, as the money was better.

Other staff

Steven Dean's father Pat was a conductor/driver on
United Counties buses, and his mother, as Cathleen
McGowen, was a conductress. He remembers that one
of the Inspectors was Harry (Sam) Cockerill.

Finally, Edwin Horner was a driver at
Northampton, while Gerald and Gilford Horner both
worked for United Counties.

Derngate Reunion, 3 May 2008

Organised by Tom Kehoe and Geoff Heginbotham
with help from Pat Dean, Frank Duffy, Paul Barnes
and their friends and families, this event was
attended by 170 bus people and their relatives at the
Northampton Working Men's Club in Sheep Street.
Commemorating 32 years and 2 days since the demise
of Derngate Bus Station, it was an
occasion to meet with colleagues and
friends, some of whom had not seen
each another since they parted more
than 30 years ago.

Most of the staff moved across
to the new bus station at Greyfriars,
while some had retired or moved on
to other jobs before the end came.

Fathers and sons, husbands and wives, office staff
and engineers came together for a catch-up session,
and many had brought photographs and their old
equipment and badges from the job.

The event took eight months to organise and
colleagues from Corby, Kettering and Wellingborough
came by coach. Some came from Bristol, Burton-on-
Trent and North Wales.

The hall was decorated in green and white, the
nearest colours to the old company livery of green and
cream, latterly green and white. Music, an excellent
buffet and the occasional drink made for a convivial
evening, which was thoroughly enjoyed by all.

Tom Kehoe prepared a couple of displays of
photographs, and staff had a great time trying to
remember the names of the former colleagues pictured.
Some were lucky enough to see themselves.

After 5 hours of reminiscing, the party broke
up with promises to keep in touch. As a result, the
opportunity was taken to meet up regularly at the club
on the first Thursday evening of every other month,
starting in June 2008, to talk about old times and
support each other.

5
Greyfriars Bus Station

Northampton's Greyfriars Bus Station replaced Derngate in 1976.

David Shadbolt

From 1986 David was Area Manager for United Counties Northamptonshire and, having no office, he moved to Greyfriars Bus Station in Northampton. At that time he remembers a great team, including Paul De Santis, Howard Butler, Jeannie Warwick and Mary Edge in the office at Greyfriars. He also remembers the Waybill Section at Northampton, which, under the leadership of Frances Piercy, had nearly 100 staff working at the office and at home, processing all the waybills.

When the United Counties company was bought by Stagecoach Holdings in 1987, David moved to a job as Commercial Manager at London Country North West, back in the south again at High Wycombe and Amersham. There he worked with Clive King, with whom he now works again at Arriva at Luton.

David then moved to become Traffic Manager at privatised company Viscount at Peterborough, Spalding, Wisbech and Oundle, and was subsequently joined by John Tate, who also moved to Viscount.

While David was at Viscount, Graham Cumming and other employees bought out Luton & District,

and in 1991 David became Commercial Manager at Hitchin and Stevenage, by then part of the Luton & District group. The sale of Luton & District to British Bus in 1993 led to another reorganisation and, with Peter Harvey at the helm, David then moved to work as General Manager at High Wycombe once more.

In 1995 David was invited by Trevor Petty, the Managing Director, to attend an interview at Midland Red North. This was where David had his first official marketing job, becoming the Marketing Manager at Cannock, marketing the company's services to its customers. As a result of this job, he was able to get a job back in the Luton area with Arriva the Shires as Marketing Manager, dealing with publicity and the media. If a spokesperson was needed, on any subject, David was the man.

In 2000 Catherine Mason arrived as the Marketing and Customer Services Director for Arriva UK operations, and David was recruited to her team. Since then he has been an important part of the small central team, delivering marketing initiatives across the UK for all Arriva bus operations, including the award-winning 'Going your way' campaign.

David is a Northamptonshire lad and still lives with his family near his original home in East Northamptonshire.

Ann Dunkley

Ann left school and went to work at Mansfield Smith & Jones in Northampton, attending a day-

Greyfriars staff. Back row (l-r): Tony Townsend, Jeannie Warwick, Barry Warner, Malcolm Cox, Ray Wakeling and Cedric 'Sid' Quayle. From row: Bill Smith, Peter Clack, Terry Sweeney and David Shadbolt. *Northampton Chronicle & Echo*

release course at Northampton Technical College. After marriage and two sons, she returned to work as a part-time engineering clerk at the Central Works in Northampton, working for Barry Warner, the Fleet Manager, who she felt was a good boss. This job lasted from 1986 to 1988.

Colleagues she remembers from those days are Jeannie Warwick, Colin Stockley, Brian Baraclough from Bedford, and Colin Stafford. She also remembers John Tate, as he used to do three jobs: his main job was Fleet Manager, then General Manager, and also a part-time job as loose bag postman, due to his roaming around to all the depots.

At the Bedford Road offices no expense was spared in the reception area. Ann occasionally did reception duties and remembers that there was a large green marble staircase leading to the next floor. Ann worked in the accounts office and commercial office, and remembers that the Chief Clerk was Bharat Rathod, the Depot Supervisor was Rod Davies, and Bob George did driving and scheduling.

When United Counties moved bus stations to Greyfriars, Ann went as well, and has been there now for 20 years. She is now secretary to the Assistant Operations Manager (Matt) and Operations Manager (Mark Butler). Her other colleagues have dwindled to just one other clerk. Jeannie Warwick also moved to Greyfriars from Derngate, and did the overs and unders and National Express work, which ceased in 1993. Jeannie worked for United Counties and Stagecoach for all her career, as did her husband Roger. Only drivers are contracted to National Express now.

Other colleagues she remembers were Bill Sye, who now works for First Bus at St James, Northampton; Howard Butler, Commercial and Admin officer; Wendy Flinders, from central wages at Rothersthorpe Avenue; Janet Dunkeley at Rothersthorpe Avenue, Greyfriars and Kettering; Marge Boshell at Derngate and Greyfriars lost property and switchboard; Terry Gordon, conductor and cashier, who retired in 1997; Dave Slinn, Mobile Inspector and now a Revenue Protection Officer; and Johnny Appleton, who also worked his full career for United Counties.

Ann's main work also includes recruitment forms for potential new employees, administration work, stationery ordering and supply, tendering for work, admin work and the accident book. Her other colleague is Andrew Fawcett, who does shorts and holidays, while part-timers include Steve Chambers, who is a detailer.

Ann remembers that in 1986 few drivers were under 30 years old, whereas now they can be any age over 18, with very few longer-serving drivers; many are now coming to the job from careers in other professions or jobs.

Social occasions are now less, due to outside commitments by staff and lack of commitment to the clubs and societies that used to exist, although Christmas events still take place occasionally.

Howard Butler

Howard was born in Brighton and is therefore a Tilling man through and through. His father worked for British Railways, but instead of following him Howard started work, in 1961, at 55 Broadway, London, for London Transport (LT), in the bus stop placement section. LT had pet RT/RTL buses used for staff outings, with souped-up engines, and RFs and RFWs on private hires until 1964, when an overtime ban stopped this work.

Howard moved to the Publicity Office, in charge of all bus information for LT, then all tube information, and was finally in charge of the combined section, with four offices and a bill store at the Central Works.

In the meantime, in 1972 the Butlers had moved to Northamptonshire, which was Howard's parents' home area, settling in Stamford. Howard became used to visiting the family for holidays and was able to explore the United Counties buses in the town. He used to commute to London daily, taking 4 hours

Right: **Howard Butler hard at work in his office at Greyfriars Bus Station in 1992.** *Bob George, Steve Loveridge collection*

out of the day. During this time he met up with regulars in the bus preservation movement and they whiled away their journeys exchanging gossip. From these journeys he got to know Graham Ledger, owner of a preserved former United Counties Bristol KS.

In the early 1980s Howard's section at LT underwent reorganisation prior to privatisation, and he decided to leave. He contacted Rod Davies at Greyfriars Bus Station, and in due course Rod offered him a job; with his recent HGV qualification, he drove the Mobile Roadshop when required.

Howard became very busy and Bob George came to work with

Above right: **Bob George at his happiest with one of his favourite buses.** *Steve Loveridge collection*

Below: **Howard's trainer, Brian Barton, at Woburn with the former Southdown training bus, one of the 'pets'. Also on the right are Simon Mobbs, Derrick Warboys and David March, all from Kettering.** *Steve Loveridge collection*

him. Rod, Howard and Bob worked out the rotas and produced working and public timetables. Rod decided that Howard should have a PSV licence and sent him off to train with Brian Barton at Kettering on Bristol FS 718. At that time he also became friends with John Appleton, former Wellingborough driver and now owner of many former United Counties buses. After many cups of tea, he passed his test. This qualification became useful much later, when he was with Steve Loveridge and Graeme Carr, who operated

and still operate the pet vehicles in the fleet. Initially this was one of the former LT Routemasters in 1988, so Howard felt at home. Later he also felt at home when the pet buses were the former Southdown PD1 training buses.

The latest pet buses, in 2008, are two former Eastern Counties Bristol FLFs, initially painted in Royal livery and now in Stagecoach colours. These were initially used on occasional Saturday services, contracts and private hires, but the Saturday work ceased with the mass use of the latest electronic ticket machines.

In the 1980s all the drivers felt they could talk with confidence to their office colleagues, as the latter knew the work involved in the driving job and would help to sort out problems to keep the job going.

From his Greyfriars days Howard remembers Inspectors Malcolm Cox, Reg Hilliard, Norman Brown and Steve Chambers. All but Steve have now retired or moved on to other jobs.

Some of Howard's driving was with National Express coaches. At that time he used to cover on the Bradford to Gatwick expresses, which changed drivers at Rothersthorpe Services on the M1 motorway, at either 2.00am or 2.00pm. If the 2.00am driver did not sign on, Howard was woken up and sent down to cover the trip, arriving back in the afternoon.

In 1999 Roger Warwick retired from the Commercial Department at Rothersthorpe Avenue

and Howard became part of that team, with Steve Loveridge, Ray Ramsey and Graham Carr. Phillip Norwell came to head the team, from Eastern Counties, when Cambus was formed. When Cambus separated out again, he went back and Adam Rideout came in to head the team, and he is still there doing the same job. Steve Loveridge produced the schedules and these were passed over to Howard to produce the working timetable, which was registered with the Traffic Commissioners, and the public timetable.

Howard still worked the occasional driving shift when staff were absent, until his retirement in 2006. He still works on the timetables, but now at home, going in to Rothersthorpe Avenue when needed.

Andrew Fawcett

Andrew is married to Sandra, and first met her when they both worked for Scottish & Newcastle Brewery at its offices in Bedford Road, Northampton. Sandra now works at Head Office in Rothersthorpe Avenue, while Andrew started with the company in 1995 as a part-time telephone enquiry clerk.

Andrew wanted to work for the buses and did his work experience in 1993 for John Broughton (a former United Counties management trainee) at Northampton Corporation Transport (NCT). In 1995 he applied to join that company, but NCT had no vacancies, so he applied to United Counties and was

Some of Northampton's many busmen at a staff meeting. Included are Joe Takkou, Ray Walton, Gerry York, Anwar, Tommy Kehoe, Rose Witts, Bob George, Danny Kerr, Arthur Hogben, Alan Hall, Terry Sweeney and Ron Williams.
Northampton Chronicle & Echo

taken on by Rod Davis, who was brilliant with the charting and scheduling of services.

Andrew's office was small, shared with three others under the watchful eye of Bill Nicholson. Andrew was trained in the Travel Shop to cover lunchtimes with Bill Nicholson and Roger Todd, and did this work for 2-2½ years. He was trained to drive, then became an Inspector in 1998. At this time he also was trained, by Jeannie Warwick, in the workings of the Traffic Office. He also worked with Nick Stearn at the Travel Office.

One special project on which Andrew worked was a new Saturday service to Banbury. He was in charge of route learning and had a great few days travelling to Banbury and back three times.

He has also covered driving turns, fuelling vehicles, cleaning them and inspecting. One driving turn was to travel up to Manchester and bring back vehicles to replace those lost in a fire at Biggleswade Depot. Another of Andrew's jobs was to cover rest days and sickness on the prestigious X5 Oxford to Cambridge

service. He has also driven National Travel services to London and Birmingham.

When Jeannie Warwick retired, Andrew took over her work full-time. He and Ann Dunkley now cover all the administration work at Greyfriars Bus Station. Northampton now has 190 drivers, who require much clerical work to be done.

Bill Nicholson

Bill has worked for the company for 41 years, having started in 1966. After retiring from a career in conducting and driving in 1994, Bill now works in the Travel Shop in Northampton with Tricia Nugent. He was OMO driver No 11.

Bill has worked with Ray Wakeling and retired staff on outings. Day trips were organised, mainly in the 1960s and 1970s, when three coaches used to go to Brighton annually. He remembers older colleagues Ron Faulkner and Ron Garron, who had a

Another staff meeting, in 1980, with Bill Nicholson in white shirt and glasses in the second row. Others present include, on the front row, Nigel Wiggins, Mick Mullins, Henry Hall, Bob George, Alan Hall and Ron Williams. On the second row are Joe Takkou, Peter Clack, Clive Perryman and Mick Clack. Behind them are other staff members, including Les Smith, Bill Mahoney, Brian Wakefield, Pat Davis, Len Frost, Roger Bason, Roy Baxter, Des Banyard and Sharif. *Northampton Chronicle & Echo*

Bill is in uniform fifth from the left in this photograph of a retired staff outing, which **included a stop at Rutland Water. The other driver was Lenny Davenport.** *Bill Nicholson collection*

friendly rivalry; every time Ron G. brought a bus into Northampton, Ron F. would wind the seat down so that Ron G. would have to see through the steering wheel rather than the window. These were the 'Two Rons', compared with the 'Two Ronnies' on the BBC.

Bill remembers that there was a Busmen's Social Club in Newland Street, and that the Swan Pub was a busman's pub. Other colleagues he remembers were Peter Clack and Max Jones from the Telephone Enquiry Unit and Travel Shop from 2000.

Ken Hall

Ken started as a driver in Kettering in 1988, but since 2006 he has been the Stagecoach Northants Publicity man. His job entails making sure that all the bus stops are up-to-date, and most recently making Northampton's bus stops into 'BUZZ' stops.

Ken sets up the bus stops on routes that are either new, or have been rerouted. For this work he uses the Stagecoach Camper Van, one of the L-registration minibuses converted as a workshop/mobile unit. It has curtains to stop his stock of vinyls from perishing or going out of shape.

Ken enjoys his job as it has more flexibility than a driving job. He works with Adam Rideout (Stagecoach East Publicity Manager) and has a colleague, James Rolfe, based at Bedford.

David Pike

Written in December 2008, the following contains extracts first published in the *Bristol Passenger* magazine.

None of us can choose the era in which we live and I have often wished that I have been able to seek employment 'on the buses' during the 1970s, when I first developed an interest in buses.

My first bit of luck was being born in 1961, which meant that I was old enough to become a conductor with East Kent, my local bus company. My first conducting was in the summer of 1980 at Thanet Depot, working on the 49/50/52 'round the island' group of services, using AEC Regents, Daimler Fleetlines and the occasional Bristol VRT.

My next job, the following summer, was spent 'on the back', working from Camberwell Depot of London Transport. This involved conducting on Routemaster buses working routes 3, 35, 68 and 159. I also worked on route 172, where two-door DM buses were used, and I had to work under the special conditions issued for these vehicles. At this time I passed my PSV test through an independent company at Reading.

By the summer of 1982 I was working for OK Services of Bishop Auckland in County Durham, following an advertisement in *Buses* magazine for seasonal drivers. I was lucky as they employed me under the age of 21, which was unusual in those days. Most of the vehicles were Leyland types. However, they also had two former London Transport Bristol LH buses, used on local services in the Newfield and Witton Park areas of the town and also on evening services on quiet runs, early in the week.

Next came full-time administrative work with Northampton Transport, from 1983 to 1986. However, office staff were allowed to drive and conduct and I became familiar with the Alexander and East Lancs-bodied Bristol VRTs and the Bristol LH midibuses. I was privileged to driver the three senior buses of the Daimler CVG6 type, which were still in operation. Special mention must also be made of my driving a United Counties Bristol RELL vehicle, NBD 310F, which was borrowed for a couple of days to overcome a vehicle shortage.

The looming spectre of deregulation caused me to rethink the benefits of full-time employment in the bus industry, and I sought work elsewhere. I was,

however, able to benefit from United Counties taking over all of Northampton Transport's Sunday work in 1986, enabling me to join them as a part-time driver.

Most of the driving I have done at Northampton has been on weekend late duties, often doing the same duty regularly. For a long time a late Sunday duty involved the 17.15 X64 to Corby. The bus had come through from Birmingham and connections were made at Corby with a Viscount bus for Peterborough. The Viscount bus was based at Oundle and very often the driver was Philip Norwell, who later worked on the commercial side at Northampton and is now Commercial Director at Cambridge.

Other regular runs were the contracts for Beacon Bingo in St James. At one time four or five buses ran at about 22.00 to the likes of Kettering, Rugby, Bedford, Milton Keynes and around the town.

Northampton had a share in the Cambridge-Oxford X5 service from its inception until about 2004. In later years I regularly worked the late Sunday duty,

Bristol RELL 310 arrives at the Woburn Bus Rally in 1986. David is not driving this time.
Steve Loveridge collection

which finished with the 21.05 Oxford-Milton Keynes journey. When coaches with toilets were introduced it was too complicated to base one at Northampton, so we lost our share of the service. For a time we also did most of the X2 Bedford service, and on Sundays this went on as an X30 to Cambridge. There is not much out of town work at Northampton on a Sunday now.

Once I was known at Bedford I regularly went there on loan when they were very short of staff in around 2002/03. As well as X5s I did town services and runs to Luton and Biggleswade. More recently I have gone on loan to Kettering and done X4s and a few trips to Desborough on the 19.

I have enjoyed all the buses I have driven except the Mercedes minibuses, and I'm not keen on the early low-floor Darts. The later Darts are, however, fine buses. Particular favourites were the VRs. The last batch of Volvo Olympians (S-reg) were also excellent buses, as are the B10 buses that have come more recently and are used on the Leicester X7.

I have been with this company for 22 years at the time of writing, and have just received my first long service award. The main vehicles used were Bristol VRTs.

The Northampton Depot of United Counties appeared to be favoured with new vehicles, in comparison to other depots in the company, which I believe was due to the competition from Northampton Transport.

From 1993 the Leyland Olympians began to oust the VRs and I had to ask favours of the Inspectors to be allocated a VR for my turns. This would usually be granted, as it would stop other drivers moaning about having these old buses. The last Northampton VR left in 1998. I well remember my last trip to Higham Ferrers on OVV 849R, which was the oldest one in the depot. The following year Kettering Depot's Bristol VR 941 was at Northampton, and the Inspector kindly changed the ticket machine to a Northampton one, so that I could use the vehicle.

The aforementioned 849 moved from retirement at Northampton to school contracts at Bedford, and was even painted in Stagecoach livery for the purpose. I was able to get a drive

David and a colleague discuss their next trip at Herne Bay.
David Jenkins

once again on the Sharnbrook School run before the bus retired again for good in 2002.

All was not lost, however. Not only did Northampton retain an allocation of X-registered Leyland ECW Olympians, but also in 2002 two very special buses arrived in the town from Eastern Counties at Peterborough – Bristol FLF6Gs 552, the open-topper, and 553, in original form. Their arrival and my recruitment to the panel of drivers and conductors allowed me to maintain an association with the Bristol marque, even following the demise of the ECW Olympians (buses that I never liked when they were new, but which grew on me later).

I have been fortunate to take one or other of the FLFs to the Herne Bay Rally in Kent on several occasions, and also to participate in running days at Swindon and Cheltenham arranged by the Stagecoach Group companies in those areas.

The Bristol FLF has always been my firm favourite and little did I suspect that, when I rode on one in Bristol in 1984, I would still be driving one 25 years later. The opportunity to use Bristol

FLFs on ordinary service is now restricted by the use of modern ticket machines. However, there is still scope for work at the Northampton Balloon Festival, Harpole Scarecrow Festival and for switching on the lights in Northampton, by carrying the local theatre's pantomime cast with 552.

Mark Butler

Mark left school and had a career in the Army as a policeman before retiring back to Mansfield in 1994. He then became a bus driver for Stagecoach, working at Mansfield, Retford, Worksop, Swindon and Stroud before going to Upton Park in London.

He remembers that one Friday all the buses were taken off the road at Mansfield by the Ministry. Mark and his colleagues spent all weekend going to Grimsby, Hull and Newcastle for replacement vehicles. Two buses he remembers driving were 401, a single-decker, and double-deckers 301-325, which were Olympians; 315 was named 'The Ship', 310 'The Ghost Bus', and 321 was 'Dusty Bin'.

Working up the ranks, Mark became an Inspector at Mansfield and Assistant Manager at Chesterfield before it was sold to Yorkshire Traction. He moved to Northampton in 2003 as Operations Manager.

For his 40th birthday his family surprised him with a Stagecoach bus cake.

Mark is an enthusiast as well as a career busman and was looking forward to the impending battle with First Bus in Northampton. At the time of writing he has moved on to Stagecoach Lincolnshire.

Matt Cooper

Matt is now the Operations Manager at Greyfriars Bus Station. From 1990 to 1996 he worked with High Wycombe buses, then from 1996 to 1999 he worked for MK Metro while at University, then became a management trainee. In his first year he set up Billing Aquadrome outstation, with eight buses and 15 staff. From 1999 Matt worked for First Buses in Northampton and came to Stagecoach (United Counties) in 2005.

Matt enjoyed working with Mark Butler and deputising for him when he was away. He enjoys the special occasions, such as the bus service at Silverstone Grand Prix weekend. Any buses going on the course have to be pressure-washed daily to make sure that they do not drop oil on the track.

Matt is also an enthusiast and met Roger Warwick and David Pike through their shared interest. He edited the newsletter for the Midland Counties PSV Society until it closed down.

Finally, a story from the ***Chronicle & Echo*** by Alec Brown about police officer Ian Knott, who became a bus driver for a while:

A man from Milton Keynes decided to drive himself home one night from Northampton, and stole a double-decker bus from Greyfriars Bus Station.

The bus was first noted passing through Milton Malsor at 50 miles per hour and was chased by police through Ashton, Hartwell and into Hanslope. It turned and smashed through wooden gates before

Mark Butler's own Stagecoach bus. *Mark Butler collection*

being driven on to a rugby pitch. It then collided with garages and railings as it left the pitch and wrote off two parked cars. Carrying on, the bus collided with another parked car and was pushing a fourth one along in front of it before the driver bailed out.

PC Knott ran alongside the bus and climbed through a window before pulling on the handbrake and bringing it to a halt. The bus stopped in the garden of a house, narrowly avoiding the side wall.

The Police Constable was congratulated by his bosses, and the bus company was relieved to get its bus back. As a result, security at Greyfriars was stepped up.

The moral of the story was that the driver should have been on a United Counties driving test before trying out this feat.

Finally, we see Northampton's 'Mother Christmas', who raised much money for local charities during her working life. She was Rosemary Wesley, who worked in the offices.
Northampton Chronicle & Echo

Index